Please return/renew this item by the
last date shown to avoid a charge.
Books may also be renewed by phone
and Internet. May not be renewed if
required by another reader.

www.libraries.barnet.gov.uk

LONDON BOROUGH

D1320816

INDIA UNIFORM NINE

INDIA UNIFORM NINE

SECRETS FROM INSIDE A
COVERT CUSTOMS UNIT

MARK PERLSTROM
AND DOUGLAS WIGHT

ICON

Published in the UK in 2022
by Icon Books Ltd, Omnibus Business Centre,
39–41 North Road, London N7 9DP
email: info@iconbooks.com
www.iconbooks.com

Sold in the UK, Europe and Asia
by Faber & Faber Ltd, Bloomsbury House,
74–77 Great Russell Street,
London WC1B 3DA or their agents

Distributed in the UK, Europe and Asia
by Grantham Book Services,
Trent Road, Grantham NG31 7XQ

Distributed in Australia and New Zealand
by Allen & Unwin Pty Ltd,
PO Box 8500, 83 Alexander Street,
Crows Nest, NSW 2065

Distributed in South Africa
by Jonathan Ball, Office B4, The District,
41 Sir Lowry Road, Woodstock 7925

Distributed in India by Penguin Books India,
7th Floor, Infinity Tower – C, DLF Cyber City,
Gurgaon 122002, Haryana

ISBN: 978-178578-889-5

Typeset in Adobe Garamond by Marie Doherty

Printed and bound in Great Britain
by Clays Ltd, Elcograf S.p.A.

For Sara,
who saved and transformed my life.

CONTENTS

AUTHOR'S NOTE

This book is written in honour of all frontline Customs officers and is dedicated to the memory of investigator Peter Bennett QGM, who, on 19 October 1979, was shot and killed in London while on an anti-smuggling operation.

Throughout the book, in order to protect the identities of certain individuals, some names have been changed and background details altered where necessary. Cases that exist on public record, however, are reported in their original detail.

Ten per cent of Mark Perlstrom's income generated by the book will be donated to Leukaemia UK.

PROLOGUE

Sunday 9 October 1988

I was woken by the noise of the phone ringing.

It was 3am. Something wasn't right.

'India Uniform Nine?'

It was Control. Who else called at 3am?

'Operation C-Chase has been knocked. We'll ring back in ten.'

Shit. I knew it. Bloody Americans. They must've gone early. I jumped out of bed and got dressed as quickly as I could.

I assumed US Customs jumped the gun. They had spent the last two years conducting one of the biggest, most expensive undercover operations of all time, involving agencies around the world in Panama, Paris, London and Pakistan. It was a takedown organised with military precision. The agents had their orders, everyone was primed. What had gone wrong at the eleventh hour?

It was one hell of a sting. In Tampa, Florida, dozens of the world's most notorious drug smugglers and their bag men – the money launderers – were attending a lavish wedding. Some were bringing along their wives and families; others were flying solo, hoping for a weekend of fun and some action. They were going to see some of that all right. They had no idea what was waiting

1

for them. The whole wedding was a sham. A very elaborate sham. The happy couple? Two American undercover Customs agents. The groom? The crooks knew him as Bob Musella, a money mover with Mob connections. In reality he was Robert Mazur. Like me, he was a Customs agent, but one who for the last two years had been deep undercover working his way higher and higher up the tree until he was in a position to bring down those closest to the very top of the feared Medellín cocaine-smuggling cartel, run by the most notorious criminal in the world, Pablo Escobar. One wrong move could have blown his cover and brought the whole operation crashing down.

My role in all of this was as part of a team set to arrest the UK target, known as Tango One. Asif Baakza, an official with the Bank of Credit and Commerce International London (BCCI), knowingly laundered thousands of dollars of drug money. At least he thought he had. What he didn't know was that the money he moved was actually US taxpayers' cash. That wouldn't save him though. The cartel member he was know-ingly dealing with was Mazur himself. And Mazur claimed he had been up front and told Baakza it was drugs money. It was a classic case of *mens rea* – a guilty mind. His intention to commit the crime would be enough to convict.

For months my unit, the Uniforms – a newly-formed Customs team set up to combat money laundering – monitored his house and place of work, looked at his financial status and tax returns and checked his passport applications for any aliases. Colleagues had also been investigating Tango Two, Ziauddin Ali Akbar, and his colleague Nazir Chinoy, who flitted between London and Paris.

We were a crime-fighting agency formed to act on new anti-money laundering legislation to target major drug smugglers at home and abroad, utilising far-reaching investigative tools for evidence gathering, to obtain convictions in court and to seize cash and assets.

We worked with Alpha – one of the most powerful civil service units in the country, who were able to intercept suspects' phone calls – a unit with so much muscle the police were jealous.

You might think the police were the UK's number-one law enforcement agency. You'd be wrong. Part of Her Majesty's Treasury, we were driven by a far higher motivational force than just fighting crime … we went after the money.

There had been a high-speed car chase and even a break-in to an empty office block so we could keep better surveillance on specific targets during the investigation. Now that we were at the point of arrest though, the last thing we needed was any kind of complication.

There was always a suspicion that the Americans would jump the gun with their arrests and not bother telling us. We never took anything for granted. All I could think was what if Baakza was spooked and had fled his house? Could you imagine the fall-out? A massive international operation and we lost one of Pablo Escobar's bankers? It didn't bear thinking about.

This was why I had asked Steve Berry, a senior officer and one of our most experienced operatives, to spend the night outside the target's house. If the target tried to flee, Steve was waiting for him.

But he was on his own. What if the target had spotted him and escaped by a back route? Should I have been there? This would be a colossal cock-up. I could see the headlines. 'Massive Sting Operation – Brits Lose Drugs Banker'.

I wouldn't know what happened, if anything, until Control phoned me back. I got ready to leave then waited impatiently, pacing the floor.

The phone rang again. At least I was more awake than I was ten minutes ago.

'Tango One has been arrested. Proceed to his HA.'

I could breathe more easily. That was code for Baakza's home address, a modest semi-detached house in Brent Cross, north London. He must have made a run for it. Probably thought he had a chance. I could picture Steve pouncing the moment he stepped out the front door. He'd be on his way to Bishopsgate Police Station where my boss and I would begin questioning him about what he knew about his nefarious clients. Who else did the BCCI bank do business with? From what we'd discovered they were not fussy about who opened an account with them.

I was still very much in the dark though about what had happened that night. With the Uniforms information was only passed on a need-to-know basis. We kept phone calls brief. Who knew who could be listening? We knew all too well how easy it was to bug a line.

What I did know was that for Baakza to flee he must have got a call. That could only mean the US takedown had been to some degree successful.

I left my digs in Tottenham. The streets were practically deserted. At that time on a Sunday morning, I expected nothing else. It was probably what Baakza was praying for, that he could have slipped away into the night.

In twenty minutes, I arrived at the banker's house. If everything had gone to plan I'd have been there at 6 for the knock at 7.30am. Joining me would've been my immediate boss Bruce

Letheran. He'd been the link with the Americans. A nice little number, as it meant he'd been back and forth to Florida making sure everything ran smoothly for Mazur. Now, with the Tango arrested, it was a waste of time him meeting me there.

Steve was long gone with the suspect. The Americans claimed he was already bang to rights. Mazur got him on tape and had his own receipt from the cash transfer, but we wanted to find more evidence of the transaction so there was less room for his lawyer to claim it was a stitch up.

As I arrived, the house was a hive of quiet industry. A couple of officers stood outside, while I suspected others were inside beginning their search. I stepped into what was an otherwise unremarkable semi in a London suburb. It was handy for the Tube. Brent Cross Shopping Centre was visible from the window. I was not sure what I expected from a criminal banker. Ostentatious furniture? Some garish artworks? The house was probably rented as there were few signs of a personal touch; no picture frames or bookshelves.

I briefed the team on what to look for. Any computers, diaries, Filofaxes, personal files, we'd take all that. If there was $100,000 in notes stuffed under the mattress we'd take that too. But from what we'd seen from watching Baakza for the past few months there would be none of that. He looked like the meticulous sort. A creature of habit. He left home at the same time every day, returned at the same time. Hardly had a social life. Any family must have been back home in Pakistan. He was a nothing-to-see-here sort of bloke. If Mazur hadn't been tipped his name, we'd have been none the wiser.

After briefing the team there was nothing for me to do, so I headed into the office at Custom House. It was still early, but technically the clock was ticking, as now Baakza had been arrested we only had 24 hours to question before we had to charge or release him. He'd have called his lawyer and we wouldn't begin our questioning until early afternoon. That gave us time to see what we could find at his house – and what we could unearth when we raided the offices of BCCI.

I arrived at the office in Custom House, by the River Thames, to find our chief, Walter Smith, 'Uniform One', the Senior Investigating Officer, kicking off.

'They've fucked us,' he said, the vein on his bald head looking like it was about to burst. 'Fucking Yanks have done it again.'

Geoff Heslop, our big boss, was in America for the planned press conference following the arrests. Given the time difference, he must have been sleeping.

Bruce arrived and, while I looked to him for explanation, I was not expecting much from the usually taciturn Cornishman.

'Von Raab, the US Customs Director, did a deal with one of the big TV networks,' he said. 'They went early.'

'And didn't think to tell Heslop?' I asked.

'We've been had over…'

'It's a good job Steve was there,' Walt said.

'So, he made a run for it then?' I still didn't have the full story of what happened in the early hours.

'Didn't half,' Walt said. 'Steve got him on the front lawn.'

'Where do you think he was heading?'

'Who knows? To the bank to start shredding, or to Heathrow?' replied Walt. 'You can ask him when you interview him. Before you do that, though, there's another bloody issue.'

'What's that?' Bruce said.

'We need a new search warrant,' Walt shook his head in disbelief. 'We've got the wrong bloody bank address.'

Bruce shot me a look as though it was my fault. Was it? I was sure I double and triple checked it.

'Steve noticed it when he got the banker to confirm his address. Turns out BCCI has two buildings next door to each other in Leadenhall Street and they're linked.'

To be fair, Customs didn't usually have this issue. Normally, when we were searching for goods subject to seizure, like drugs or booze where the tax has not been paid, Customs had a power called the Writ of Assistance. Dating back hundreds of years and signed by the monarch when he or she takes office, it is essentially a universal search warrant that is in place until said monarch dies. No other law enforcement agency in the world had it and the police hated us for it. Unfortunately, on that Sunday morning we were simply searching for documents, so the Writ of Assistance didn't extend to that.

Luckily, we had a friendly duty magistrate we could access 24 hours a day, who lived in a penthouse in the Barbican with a £37,000-a-year service charge, so Bruce and I headed there and up the twenty floors to her flat. Raising an eyebrow at the reason for our early-morning call, she signed the warrant and we headed back to the office.

'Right, let's get to the bank,' Walt said.

It was time to raid the offices of BCCI. We had been through our respective roles the day before. My job was to search Baakza's desk and cabinets.

As we prepared to leave, I saw another group of agents heading out with us, led by another very senior officer, a Scottish guy called Ian Stewart. The team had been involved in the operation up till now, but I'd never seen someone so senior on the ground before.

'What the hell is he doing here?' I asked.

'You'll see in due course,' Trevor Jardine, another senior officer, replied.

'What?'

He put a finger to his lips.

As we made the short journey by foot, our echoing steps the only noise in the city at that hour on a Sunday, I realised we were two teams on two distinct missions. There were about 30 of us, evenly split.

We descended on the main entrance of BCCI, at 100 Leadenhall Street. It was all shut up and, save for a couple of security guards at the desk inside, the place was deserted. In we piled.

'UK Customs,' Walt announced. 'We have a warrant to search the offices of Asif Baakza.'

One of the guards took the form and entered some details into his computer.

'His office is next door. You can access the building that way,' the guard said, pointing to a connecting door.

We strode though the door, into a plush, mustard-coloured, open-plan workspace, admiring the extensive smoked-glass windows through which the morning light was starting to seep in. I couldn't help compare it to the asbestos-riddled shithole we called home.

We found Baakza's desk. Nothing fancy, just one of dozens that all looked the same. There were no pictures of children, no funny ornaments or corporate tat, just a functioning workspace. Either the guy was a robot, or he knew he might have to ditch this desk in a hurry one day.

I tasked the team to look for evidence of the Mazur/Musella transaction, any ledgers, or paperwork referring to $10,000.

Ian Stewart and his team focused on the desk and cabinets

next to Baakza's. What did he know? There was no point asking. As with all Uniform activity it was on a need-to-know basis.

It didn't take us long to find what we were looking for – a yellow ledger card, clearly for the right transaction. It wasn't crucial, but it would be helpful when we came to question the banker.

I got the impression Ian also found what he was looking for, as there were satisfied nods all round on his team. What could it have been? Over the past months we'd realised that BCCI was no ordinary bank, but Ian's presence suggested something on a whole new level. Who else did they bank for? Was there anyone they wouldn't do business with?

I left the team to finish the search, as it was time Bruce and I headed to Bishopsgate to finally meet Baakza. It was funny. During all the time we had kept this man under surveillance, monitoring his movements, who he met, where he shopped, where he ate, I couldn't help but feel sorry for him. He struck me as any ordinary Joe. Mazur could have chosen any banker in the City to launder his cash to show how corrupt the system was. But then, as I made my way to the interview room, my head was back to spinning. Why was such a senior officer on the raiding party?

If the focus was really on something else, something much bigger, then what was my team doing there? All that time I thought we were targeting Escobar's money, hitting the world's biggest cocaine empire where it hurt, joining forces with our US counterparts to fight the good fight. I now feared it had nothing to do with that. That we were all a by-product of something bigger.

Bruce gave me a nod. Baakza's lawyer had arrived, and they were waiting for us. It was time to find out what he knew.

I had a horrible feeling in the pit of my stomach. I had joined this unit to clean up the money launderers. Why then did I feel so dirty all of a sudden?

CHAPTER 1

Spirit of adventure

Don't take anything at face value. That's what I've always believed, and it was a mindset instilled in me by my father.

Our family was a case in point. On the face of it, ours was an average northern, working-class household. My dad worked in the steel industry, my mother was a carer in an old people's home and we lived in a typically modest two-up, two-down house, but that doesn't tell the whole story.

A bitter family argument in a small town near Stockholm a century ago dramatically shaped the course of our history. The row was enough to prompt teenager Carl Frederick Perlstrom to walk out, head straight to the nearest port and stow away on a trawler bound for Grimsby.

A local woman and her teenage daughter, enjoying a traditional prom walk at the seaside in Cleethorpes, found the young lad wandering the streets and, because he had nowhere to go, took him in. He fell in love with the teenage girl and they married a few years later, moving to Sheffield to find work.

Sadly, I never met my runaway grandfather, as he died before I was born, but the story of how he arrived on these shores has become enshrined in our family folklore. My dad inherited his father's spirit of adventure, but also discovered his Swedish heritage had unintended consequences. He wanted to join the Royal Navy, but they wouldn't let him because of his father's nationality, so he opted for the Merchant Navy instead.

When the Second World War broke out, and Britain depended on vital supplies from overseas territories and North America to survive, my dad was regularly on-board merchant ships which were vulnerable to attack by German submarines, or U-boats. As the Navy couldn't protect individual ships, they grouped them into large convoys with military escorts, the idea being they would be harder to find and more difficult to attack.

Try telling that to my dad. Twice he was on ships torpedoed by U-boats, and each time he found himself in the Atlantic, swimming for his life. I can't even imagine how frightening that would be, but it didn't put him off. After the war he stayed in the Merchant Navy and travelled all over the world. Wherever I've visited he's been. For instance, when I went to South Africa he casually remarked: 'I've sailed from Durban many times, round the Cape of Good Hope.' He told stories of hundred-metre waves and mistaking whales for submarines.

Such was his wanderlust he emigrated to New Zealand and worked in a steel factory there, but my grandmother pined so much for him that he came home to Sheffield.

Experiencing what it was like to be under attack and having an immigrant background shaped my dad's views. 'Never let anyone tell you Britain or America won the war,' he told me, when I went to school. His view was that we owed the Russians for victory. 'They lost 20 million men,' he said. 'Ordinary Russians fought the Germans with broomsticks and anything they could lay their hands on.'

He might not have a had a higher education, but he was an intelligent man and his words stuck with me, particularly when faced with a largely jingoistic narrative from my history teachers. Who's right, I thought, the history books, or my dad who experienced it?

That healthy scepticism, a distrust for authority and an instinct to question everything has remained with me. I always try to work out if the propaganda or indoctrination is correct or not. You could say anti-establishmentarianism is in my DNA.

There was, however, an element of my grandfather's heritage I could care less about. When I was born in 1961, my dad wanted to call me Carl Frederick too. My mother Maureen hated it and put her foot down. The compromise was to name me Frederick Mark Perlstrom, but call me by my middle name. This suited me fine.

My younger brother was named Carl. We have a younger sister, Jill, and, growing up, the five of us shared two bedrooms in a house with no inside toilet or bathroom in the inner-city district of Walkley. Again, that doesn't quite tell the whole story.

We have an elder sibling, Gail, who lived in the house before we were born and then went to live with our maternal grandmother, as we didn't have enough space in the tiny terrace. I would go over to my grandparents on a Sunday to visit them. Living in a council flat, she had a proper bath, which was the height of luxury back then, especially when we had to make do with a tin tub otherwise.

My paternal grandmother ran a chip shop, and for years that was the focal point of the family, with all members living nearby helping out, including Gail. Unfortunately, eating a lot of fried food from the shop was one of the reasons I was overweight.

My dad needed an English breakfast every morning because he was on his feet all day in the factory, where he worked as a turner for a steel company. It was a small, family firm that produced blades and utensils for Stanley Tools, and he turned the lathe to a fraction of a millimetre accuracy.

Those big breakfasts were the first of our four meals each day. When I started at Myers Grove School, we'd have lunch there, then a fry-up for dinner at 5pm. Mum would then go off to work at the old people's home or as a service assistant in the canteen in the children's hospital, and not return home until 10pm, by which time we'd be starving and go to the chip shop for a big supper.

When, in a biology lesson, the teacher decided to weigh the class and it emerged I was a good four-to-six stones heavier than my classmates, it hit home. I felt humiliated. No wonder I struggled to attract a girlfriend. At least I wasn't the target of bullies, but this might have been because I was the one picking on people. I received a thrashing for one ill-judged comment and my behaviour was raised in my report card.

As a result, I was a bit of a loner at school. What saved me was my love of sport. I played football, rugby and cricket at school. I enjoyed being at the stumps, until someone said I was good but not too fast between the wickets. That brought me down a little. I had a cousin who was a professional golfer, so Dad bought me a set of clubs. I didn't join a private club, as I couldn't stand the culture in such places, but there were two municipal courses in Sheffield so, on a Saturday, I'd pay £2 and play a round on my own.

Although I quite liked other sports, football was my real passion. I attended Hillsborough Boys Club, as did the few friends I had. There was a floodlit five-a-side pitch, and we'd play there until 10pm every night. A lot of kids our age went off the rails when they hit their teens and got into drinking and loitering or went joyriding, but football kept me on the straight and narrow, and I earned the nickname Pele.

One of my fondest memories was seeing my legendary name-sake playing, when his team Santos played Sheffield Wednesday in 1973. It was the second time the world's greatest player appeared in Sheffield after a previous visit five years earlier. My mates and I wagged off school to go to the game, which kicked off at 2pm on a Tuesday afternoon, because the country was on a three-day week at the time and the lights were switched off to save electricity, as coal was short due to a miners' strike.

Dad used to take me to watch both Sheffield teams, Wednesday and United, which was the done thing in those days. He even took me to London to watch United play Chelsea. He was a keen ornithologist and the real reason for the visit was to take me to an RSPB sanctuary on the Norfolk coast to go birdwatching. Afterwards we drove into London and slept in the back of our Ford Cortina estate as he wouldn't pay for a bed and breakfast. It wasn't long, however, before I focused solely on Wednesday and the Owls became something of an obsession. And all the family were Blue through and through.

When I wasn't playing football, I used to go off to the local Carnegie or Central libraries to do research, and endlessly read the *Encyclopaedia Britannica*. I loved geography and history, and would study a different American city each visit. I retained all sorts of trivial information, like that Cleveland used to be the third-biggest city in the United States, is situated in the Rust Belt, was called the 'mistake on the lake' after the decline of its steel industry and used to have a population of 4.6 million people.

I also read biographies of famous people from history, and books on sport. My parents weren't great readers, in fact I can't recall ever seeing a book in the house, until my dad picked up a 1936, gold-leafed edition of *Encyclopaedia Britannica* from a church jumble sale for £5.

I think, like a lot of men in his line of work, Dad was exhausted when he came home from work and, after being on his feet all day, just wanted to slouch in front of the television in the evening.

When I was fourteen, we moved to a bigger house in Hillsborough, near Wednesday's football ground. For the first time we had an indoor bathroom and three bedrooms, so my sister had a room of her own. However, once the utility bills started coming in my dad realised he couldn't afford to heat it. They were on low wages and had 40-a-day cigarette habits to fund. After a year we moved again, this time to a smaller house in Rivelin, but the council gave Dad a grant to install an indoor bathroom. There was only central heating downstairs, heating the kitchen and the front room. This meant the bedrooms were freezing, literally. There were often icicles hanging inside the windows. We were now a little further out from the city centre, but for Dad it was ideal as our small garden led to the bottom of the valley and the River Rivelin, where he could walk for miles trying to spot kingfishers and woodpeckers.

Growing up in such a frugal atmosphere had a profound effect on me. I craved financial security and was determined to earn enough, so I'd never go back to a house without a bathroom.

However, my first attempts to forge a career weren't too successful. Without any help from our chronically bad careers service at school I decided I would join the military, thinking the public sector might be an opportunity to continue my education as well as having a job. Each of the armed forces had a recruiting office in Sheffield, so I tried the Navy. They told me I needed to lose eight stone before they'd consider me. It was probably a blessing, as I get seasick on the ferry to Calais and wouldn't have lasted five minutes.

In 1978, I landed a job as a clerk for Niloc Tools, earning £25 a week. As soon as I got my first pay packet, I bought a £100 share in Sheffield Wednesday. I only stayed there for two months before moving to a furniture-making company on £5-a-week more as a stock auditor. For this job, I travelled the country visiting retailers in company cars, as part of a team reconciling the physical stock with the computer record. For the first time in my life, I got to stay in a hotel. Saying overnight in places like Coventry and Carlisle never felt so exciting.

I was there nearly a year when I travelled to London mid-week to take in Wednesday's match against Brentford and find a job in the capital, where I'd always wanted to live. I found a vacancy at the St Ermin's Hotel, in St James's Park, as an accounts clerk on £55 a week. Not only that but they owned their own hostels, and to stay in one only cost a fiver a week. I applied, got the job and moved to London to begin work on 2 January 1980.

The hotel was like nowhere else I'd ever been. Its location, with a division bell of Westminster, meant it was very popular with politicians who, on hearing the signal that a vote was occurring, had eight minutes to get to the Houses of Parliament to cast them.

It is where the Cambridge spy Kim Philby was recruited into MI6, and its connection to espionage literally runs deep, with underground rooms and tunnels linked to 55 Broadway, the former headquarters of the intelligence services during the war and now London Transport's HQ.

My hostel was in Earl's Court. When I arrived, I exited the Tube station and walked past shops selling kebabs and falafels and other seemingly exotic foods I'd never seen before. Even my first sight of a McDonald's felt other-worldly.

I couldn't have wished for a more wonderful introduction to London. The atmosphere in the hostel was fantastic, with dozens of hotel workers from all over the world, particularly Australia and the Philippines. The social scene was buzzing. We regularly went to a gay bar called the Copacabana, and I remember David Bowie walking in with Gary Numan and giving an impromptu concert on the tabletops. Pink Floyd played *The Wall* at the exhibition centre at the end of our road; the punks were in their element. If you took a walk down Earl's Court Road you might easily have seen Freddie Mercury, Terence Stamp or big television personalities of the day, like Russell Harty and Willie Rushton.

I joined the Sheffield Wednesday London Supporters Club, whose president then was Roy Hattersley MP, a senior Labour politician. If the Owls played in the south, I'd go along to watch, or take in the Saturday night motor bike racing over Battersea Bridge.

It felt like a different planet to Sheffield. There, I hadn't even known of an openly gay person. Now I counted many of them as friends and met so many wonderful people from all over the world, as the hotel attracted a diverse staff.

I'd been there for a year when the hotel chain began selling off its staff hostels. I moved from Earl's Court to Maida Vale, another beautiful area, where I counted Joan Collins and Richard Branson, on a houseboat, as neighbours. We had a tennis court at the back, next to Warwick Avenue Tube station. The vibe was gentile, less eclectic and very English.

|||

My job was simply to reconcile the hotel's purchases and make sure suppliers were paid, but I started to discover there were other careers out there. We had several oil companies as clients, but when I inquired about job opportunities with them I realised I didn't have the right qualifications for many roles. One oil contact advised me to consider the civil service. 'You can get in at a lower level and in the public sector there are no such things as budget constraints, so you can pretty much do what you want,' he told me. 'If you want to go on a training course, you can. If you want to study accountancy, they'll pay for it. Time management, human relations? They'll put you on a course. You never have to leave and when you retire at 60 it will be on a full final salary pension.'

At the back of my mind was still that longing for security. As much fun as I was having, I was determined not to return to an ice-cold house in Sheffield. I saw a job in the *Evening Standard* for a clerical assistant, applied and, to my surprise, got it. Little did I know that as the civil service paid so little, they were desperate for staff.

The job itself sounded grand – in the procurement executive for the Ministry of Defence (MoD). The top minister at the time was Michael Heseltine, and we were essentially buying ejector seats and other equipment for the RAF. The reality was there was very little work to do, however, it was an insightful introduction to the public sector. I was told we had a massive fictitious department that only existed on paper, with a mega budget and thousands of staff, and of course everything was so sensitive and secret no auditors were allowed near it. When the Treasury imposed cuts, it was only this ghost outfit that was reduced.

My colleagues were mainly retired RAF and Naval staff who had served in the war. Instead of pushing them out, the MoD gave them civil service jobs. They had grand titles, like Wing Commander Smith, retired, and many were suffering from what now would be diagnosed as post-traumatic stress disorder.

I loved hearing their stories from the war and the Battle of Britain. My immediate boss had been a 'Tail End Charlie', the rear gunner in a bomber, and he had lost half of his face and had to have his features reconstructed. Guys like him were phenomenally intelligent and obviously highly courageous. It was amazing just being in their company. There were also people who had worked at Porton Down, the top-secret and controversial military facilities, where they researched biological weapons.

Although I was promoted quite quickly in my MoD career, after nearly two years I had a hankering to head back north. I'd tried to buy property in London but would have to move out as far as Hastings, in Sussex, to afford a flat that even then would set me back £6,000.

Ideally I wanted to return to Sheffield, but there were no suitable vacancies there. However, in Salford, near Manchester, there was an opening that caught my eye. It was in Her Majesty's Customs and Excise, just a clerical job, but it was in the regional headquarters, or 'collection', as they called it. This was the outfit that tackled drug smugglers and big tax fraud cases.

I was into James Bond. Drug trafficking and tax investigations sounded far more interesting than the clerical work I was doing for the MoD. It was only an hour away from Sheffield, so I could go home on Friday nights and spend the weekend at home.

I didn't have to think twice. And so, in April 1985, I prepared to move to Salford. Although I was heading home, it felt like a new life was waiting.

CHAPTER 2

||||||||||||||||||||||||||||||||||||||||||||

The Customs' philosophy

'Everybody's bent, remember that. Everyone is at it. Everyone is on the make. Everyone is trying to fiddle taxes. And our job is to protect the revenue as best we can.'

Two weeks into my new job in Salford and I had joined half a dozen other new recruits for a Revenue Awareness Course. Essentially it was an indoctrination. The message? That we now worked for Customs, which was a department of Her Majesty's Treasury. The main thing we needed to be concerned about was money. Over two days, we listened to talks from representatives from the four divisions of Customs, including the VAT office, which dealt with revenue from the sales tax, and those that dealt with excise duty, the tax dating back hundreds of years primarily on alcohol and tobacco.

But it was the arrival of a senior investigator that had the biggest impact. He was from the team that occupied the top floor, the operational unit that had already achieved mythical status in my young eyes. Not only were these the guys that tackled drug traffickers, made huge seizures, caught crooks and generated big headlines for the department, but they looked a cut above everyone else.

From the host of our training session through each of the specialist speakers, the mantra was the same: 'Think revenue all the time.'

'People are basically dishonest,' the investigator said. 'You've just got to prove it. If not, that's fine, move on, but basically most people are and we can get money off them.'

The senior VAT officer, from their office a short walk away, told us to be mindful of scams 24 hours a day. 'Be aware of anything,' he said. 'If for instance you see someone selling counterfeit products, question whether they have registered for VAT.'

He explained that the easiest way to attack people in those situations was to go after them for VAT. With the cap set at £20,000, anyone earning above that should be registered.

'Is your local cricket club bar taking that amount of money?' he said. 'If so, they should be VAT registered.'

No one was safe, it seemed.

Each speaker explained to us the laws that affected each common fiddle. The biggest source of tip-offs, the VAT officer explained, was any business's main competitor.

'If you're doing a fiddle that puts you at an advantage over your rivals,' he went on, 'then they are going to contact us.'

The second most common source was bitter ex-spouses in acrimonious divorces.

'I can't tell you how many times we take calls from a recently divorced woman who says, "We had a shop down the road and my ex doesn't pay all the VAT. He's got an account in Jersey."'

The chap from the Excise office, situated a mile away, explained how the smugglers selling contraband booze and cigarettes off the back of lorries were so costly to the exchequer. We were to tip them off about anyone we saw or heard doing this.

Another issue I previously knew nothing about was red diesel. Only certain vehicles, mostly tractors and other farm equipment, were permitted to run on rebated fuel, which was coloured red, so it was easily identifiable, but a black market existed because it was cheaper. The excise investigators had just blown a big case in the Manchester area.

Equally fascinating was an officer from TIVLO, the Temporary Imported Vehicle Licensing Office.

'If you see a foreign car on the street, make a note of the registration number and the address where it is parked,' he said, 'and we will check if the owner has paid the proper import tax or road tax.' He handed out forms. 'Just fill them in, we'll do the rest.'

For a new recruit it was a startling insight. Before that course, I had considered my job to be mind-numbingly boring. All I did was buy furniture for our office and other Customs teams in Manchester collection. The office was depressing. Everything was what I called municipal mustard and green. Years later, when I visited the former headquarters of the East German Stasi secret police in Berlin, I was struck by how much it reminded me of civil service offices in the mid-eighties.

Where we were was a bit of a wasteland. The docks had closed years before, and our six-storey office block had no real amenities. It was an administrative base for the Manchester area, housing our various departments.

Suddenly, though, it felt like there was an edge to the job. I wasn't required to know any of this stuff for my role, but they were preparing us in case we transferred to investigations, and they clearly wanted to motivate the staff to do so. For the first time there was a career path I wanted to follow.

I heard stories from the Investigations Division, of drugs they'd seized from Colombia. Previously this was the type of thing I only heard on the news, now it was on my doorstep. Globally, the war on drugs was a big issue. In his first term of office US president Ronald Reagan had approved tough new legislation on drug traffickers with harsher penalties for offenders and greater powers for law enforcement.

In addition, I got sight of some of the cheques coming in from big companies for excise duties. Daily, cheques would arrive from various oil companies, for £20 million each. The amount of revenue was staggering, but the ethos was simple; potential revenue was everywhere. You had to be able to smell it.

Whalley Range, where I was living from Monday to Friday, was a notoriously rough area, but the YMCA hostel I used had only recently opened, was ideal for my purposes and was only a twenty-minute bus ride from the office. I enjoyed my time in Manchester. The locals were friendly, and I saw David Bowie and Queen perform live at Maine Road, which was then City's ground. Other events stuck in the mind for various reasons. I remember watching the shocking images from Heysel Stadium in Brussels in 1985, as Liverpool and Juventus fans clashed ahead of the European Cup final.

About a week later I was walking to my hostel when I spotted a Volvo with Swiss plates. I filled in a form the TIVLO officer had given us and sent it to his office. Two days later the officer rang me up.

'That car you spotted? They hadn't paid import duty on it. We'll received £700 for that. Well done.'

Not only that, but he called my boss to let him know what happened and he put a note in my personal file commending me for being highly motivated. I had had my first success in investigation, and somebody had said thank you and allocated credit accordingly. That was all the confirmation I needed. Investigations was the job for me.

At that stage, however, it was out of my reach. I was a lowly administrative officer. Investigators were executive officers, the grade above me. Still, with commendations like the one from TIVLO, I was on my way. I just had to get a promotion first.

After sticking out the furniture purchasing for a year, I knew I needed to move again to progress, so, when I saw a vacancy at the Sheffield VAT office, I jumped at it. It was a sideways move, but I hoped the job would be more interesting.

The position was with the enforcement team, whose role it was to go round businesses that had run up considerable VAT debts and recover the revenues they owed us.

It was a new experience, getting out and about, but obviously we weren't welcome visitors. Generally, I played second fiddle to a vastly more experienced colleague, so it was a watch-and-learn role, letting the senior people lay it on the line to the tax evaders and non-payers. Generally, though, they paid up. If not, and they had a poor compliance record, we put them into bankruptcy.

One of our jobs was to check for red diesel and I got a shock one day when an old school friend of mine came into the office to pay a tax fine. He had been there when we skipped school to see Pele. He now had a haulage company, and my colleagues had found the tax-free fuel in his personal car. They had fined him £700 and here he was paying it off at £25 a week. Funnily enough, now he's a multi-millionaire, from what I see on Facebook. Who says crime doesn't pay?

I enjoyed the job but what intrigued me more was a secondary investigative role we could volunteer for in the evenings. Test eating was where Customs allowed two officers to dine out at a local restaurant. We'd buy a meal, pay in cash with money from Customs and then wait to see if the owner declared it. If, after three months, they hadn't declared our dinner bill on their quarterly VAT return, a control officer would pay them a visit.

It was my first taste of undercover work, and involved being paid overtime and having an evening meal on the government. It only occurred to me much later that we only ever targeted restaurants owned by ethnic minorities, usually Indian or Chinese.

I was enjoying both roles and after a couple of months at home I had the security I'd craved, plus enough money saved to put a deposit on a small, terraced house in Sheffield. This was thanks to the Crown Transfer, a considerable employment benefit civil servants could take advantage of when moving house. The government paid for all moving expenses, including a portion of your mortgage that tracked the interest rate for ten years, so that you were never out of pocket. The intention behind the scheme was to ensure that your living standards did not have to drop should you have to move location due to work, but some people took advantage, moving every few years to cash in. The scheme was far more lucrative if you owned a house, rather than rented, and so I was keen to get on the housing ladder. I bought the first property I saw. It cost £17,000, but needed renovating.

I had worked in the VAT office for a few months when I saw an advert for a role at a tobacco warehouse outside Sheffield. Having got a taste, literally, of some undercover work at the restaurants, I now fancied getting some experience on the frontline. Technically, I would be moving next door to the excise office, but working at a trader's premises. Collecting the money at source felt like a fresh challenge and was good experience. Plus, a recent health scare meant I had to knock the nightly test-eating trips on the head.

I had felt a sharp pain in my heart, and when I went to my GP he said, bluntly: 'If you don't lose weight, you're dead.'

He referred me to a dietician at Sheffield Hallamshire Hospital, who told me in no uncertain terms what I needed to do to get healthy. She put me on a high-fibre diet, cutting out fried food, chocolate and alcohol. I'd had such a fright I didn't need any persuading. I started it immediately and was so disciplined the weight quickly fell off. I lost ten stone over the next year, and I've loosely stuck to it ever since.

|||

I had a brief training stint in the excise office, before moving to the warehouse in Maltby, a small, former mining town ten miles east of Sheffield city centre. It was an eye-opener. The premises, which had only been operating for eighteen months, generated £2 million a day in tobacco duty. It was what was known as a bonded warehouse, which meant the company could store products duty-free under certain circumstances.

Excise revenue never ceases to amaze me. Tax on Scotch whisky is currently 70 per cent, meaning that a £35 bottle could cost £10.50 if duty-free. That's why smuggling is such a problem. It was also why bonded warehouses are strictly controlled. There were three of us Customs employees there, making sure everything was in order. But that didn't mean frauds couldn't be committed.

The workers at the warehouse were largely ex-miners, whose livelihoods had been destroyed by Margaret Thatcher's ruinous policy of closing the coal mines. This was 1986, Sheffield had lost 70,000 jobs in the steel industry, the mines were gone and South Yorkshire was one of the most depressed areas in Western Europe. It was sad to watch these hardened men now moving boxes of fags and pallets around for a pittance.

My days were spent securing containers to be shipped. I sealed them, and when they got to their destination – Morocco, for example, or Saudi Arabia – they were stamped at the other end, confirming the products inside could be moved duty-free. With 2 million fags on each container, there were millions of pounds worth of excise duty at stake.

The first time I knew that something was amiss at the warehouse was when Customs investigators from the Birmingham Office of the national Investigation Division kicked the door in one morning. I had no idea the raid was coming. The whole Customs' philosophy is built on a need-to-know basis.

As soon as the investigators burst through the door, they started interviewing staff and seizing records from the warehouse and computers.

The staff were understandably frightened. After what they'd been through, if they lost their jobs they might never work again. However, as the investigators began their inquiries, it was clear the workers' loyalty was to the company, so they kept schtum and refused to cooperate.

As they were getting nowhere, the investigator in charge of the operation started telling the workers during questioning that the warehouse was closing, and that they were all going to lose their jobs. There was no point in them remaining loyal anymore. This had the desired effect, and they started singing and began giving formal witness statements, which helped confirm the fraud.

I got on well with one of the girls in the warehouse, and the following day she said: 'The behaviour of your guys yesterday was horrendous.'

'Why?' I asked.

'They told them they were all going to lose their jobs. It was all a lie. The warehouse is not closing. Their jobs are safe.'

I asked my boss about it and she confirmed it. 'He just made it up. It worked though. Some of them were able to be extremely helpful. That's the ID for you.'

Amazing, I thought, it was like something out of *The Sweeney*. Word was the raid netted nearly £2 million in lost revenue, so was a big success.

|||

That was my first proper introduction to the Investigation Division (ID) – the national agency of elite agents who previously had only been a source of wonder to me. All the anecdotes I heard were about their daring antics, taking on drug smugglers. Some officers had lost their lives in the course of their duties. Everybody in Customs was in awe of them. When we'd had a Customs sports day in London, where teams from all the regional offices and HQ competed against each other, it was the ID who stood out. They looked cool and had an air of superiority about them.

But by now the antics of the Investigation Division was not just confined to Customs. A new BBC television drama series, *The Collectors*, shone a light on their work like never before. Starring Michael Billington – an actor once tipped as the next James Bond after Sean Connery – as the dashing lead Customs officer, it ran for ten weeks and showed the lengths officers went to to catch criminals.

As if that wasn't enough, a seven-part documentary mini-series ran on the BBC a year later. *The Duty Men* followed investigations by Customs officers into drug and counterfeit-goods trafficking. I watched investigators called the Romeos fly from London to Australia to seize three kilos of coke and nick several drug traffickers, imagining it might be me one day.

A few weeks after the tobacco warehouse raid a promotion board was formed. This was my chance to reach the grade required to apply to be an investigator. I had to be approved for promotion before I could move up the ladder.

The Collection – regional headquarters – for Sheffield was East Midlands and the head office was in Nottingham, so it was there I had to go for an interview board.

In my most recent annual review, I'd received a good report, which meant I was now 'fitted for promotion'. With that in my favour I really would have to make a right mess of the interview board not to get a promotion.

It was a straightforward process, the interview went well and I was confident they would award me the promotion.

Running simultaneously was a recruitment drive for the Investigation Division, with vacancies mainly in the London headquarters. This was a more challenging prospect and might mean another interview for the ID.

On the application form you could say where you wanted to go. With a London HQ, the ID had five regional offices – in Glasgow, Leeds, Birmingham, Manchester and Bristol. There was also scope to apply for one of the many local units, like the Manchester Collection Investigation Unit, or CIU.

I put down all the national IDs and local CIUs in order of preference, starting with London. If you joined the ID, you immediately received a £10,000 annual allowance. With that

I could move back to the capital and, with a Crown Transfer, buy a decent flat.

My boss, who recommended me for promotion, was also an ex-investigator, and he prepped me for my interview, telling me to research new trends and legislation. Our internal magazines had several reports about new anti-money laundering legislation soon coming into practice.

The Drug Trafficking Offences Act 1986 was ground-breaking, the first time the law had been changed here to target the assets and proceeds of drug crime, not just the importations or dealing.

A popular myth is that the concept of money laundering dates back to the 1930s when notorious Chicago mob boss Al Capone was said to have bought launderettes and other cash businesses to disguise his dirty dosh. The prohibition gang-ster was famously jailed for tax evasion, but it's more likely the term was coined from machines that were literally used to clean grimy, used banknotes. The machines might have fallen out of use in the mid-20th century, but the term evolved to relate to any process of cleaning dirty, or criminally obtained, cash.

'Don't be gung-ho,' my boss said, 'play it cool with the interview panel.'

'Their favourite question is, "You've arrested someone, you've got to search his house, what do you do?"

'The hotheads will say, "Let's go and kick his fucking door in."

'Wrong answer. The right answer is to say, "Search him for the key to the front door and let yourself in, because why do you want to cause damage and aggro for someone and have to find a locksmith to repair the door?"

'They ask these types of questions to weed out the crazies. They want to decide who can do a complex fraud, who can handle a 2-million-page document investigation for a VAT fraud? Who is bright enough for money laundering? Anyone else, they can stick them on an operational drugs team.'

With that in mind – and as I asked myself whether I was cut out for a complex VAT fraud or money laundering case – I headed to the ID's head office in New Fetter Lane, off Fleet Street, for my interview.

Of around 200 applicants, I was one of the select few asked to meet the panel. When I walked in it was obvious these were three gnarled, seasoned investigators. They looked like they'd spent their career kicking down doors and had seen a lifetime's worth of action.

I was glad of my boss's advice. Most of their questions focused on the new anti-money laundering legislation and thanks to my research I was able to answer them confidently.

Funnily enough, they didn't ask the favourite question. Did this mean I had passed? Had they earmarked me for something other than drugs?

A month after the interview my boss came to see me.

'Two bits of news,' he said. 'One, you've been promoted. Two, you've got the ID in London.'

I couldn't believe what I was hearing. I had made it. I was joining the elite.

'When do I start?'

'Right away.'

He wasn't joking. It was October 1987, and, once everything had been arranged, I was due to transfer in just three weeks.

Once again, I packed my things and headed off to London. This time, however, I was joining the big league.

CHAPTER 3

‖‖‖‖‖‖‖‖‖‖‖‖‖‖‖‖‖‖‖‖‖‖‖‖‖‖‖‖‖‖‖‖‖‖‖‖‖‖‖

Joining the big league

Central London, November 1987

I had my eyes on the target. Don't lose him, I told myself for the hundredth time that afternoon. Easier said than done.

We were in central London, approaching the Natural History Museum, heading west on the A4. Traffic was slow moving, but all it took was one driver swerving out, the target jumping a red light and we could lose him. I didn't want that to happen. Not on my first operation for the ID.

At least I wasn't the 'eyeball'. That was the job of those in the car directly behind the target, or Tango One as we called him. In all, we had four vehicles tailing him. I was in the car behind the eyeball. I was a potential footman, they said. If he pulls over, I had to jump out. I turned the walkie-talkie over in my hand, reminding myself again how to use it. I didn't want to be tailing this guy on my own and not be able to radio for back-up.

Next to me, driving and navigating, was Bruce Letheran, my vastly more experienced colleague. Glancing out the window it crossed my mind how blissfully ignorant the people out there on the street were to what was going on. The pavements were crammed with visitors, kids with dinosaur souvenirs from the Natural History Museum or spaceships from the Science Museum next door. To them we probably looked like normal cars in a queue of traffic. How many of them would have believed an international drug smuggler was in their midst and on his tail an elite team of Customs investigators?

Because that's what we were. A specially assembled team to target, for the first time by Customs, money launderers ... and, occasionally, drug traffickers.

This job had come from the Canadian High Commission in Grosvenor Square. Each embassy had representatives from various law enforcement agencies and this request had come from the famous Mounted Police. They were after a British-born drug trafficker who had smuggled twenty tonnes of cannabis into Canada and was moving his cash through London. They had intelligence he was putting another run together and they wanted us to follow him, find out what he did with his money and who he met. The name they had for him turned out to be false. It was our job to correctly ID him and find out as much as we could about his operation.

So far, we'd established the hotel Tango One used. It wasn't easy. Even the more seasoned veterans said they'd never seen a target drive as fast as this guy. We'd also managed, somehow, to follow him to an address in rural Hampshire, owned and lived in by an elderly woman. Rather than try to follow him back from the Hampshire cottage and attempt a high-speed surveillance, we positioned another car on the A3 at Putney, figuring he would have to pass it on the way back to London. Once the eyeball clocked Tango One leaving the cottage in his rented three-litre Mercedes, he radioed to the next car. Even calculating for the speed the target drove, it was staggering how quickly the suspect arrived in south London.

Our chief Walt Smith guessed the woman he was visiting was his mother, and wondered whether the reason for the visit could even be a birthday. He ran what we knew of the suspect's details through CEDRIC – the Customs and Excise Departmental Research and Intelligence computer – and, sure enough, the name of the woman and the date of the visit helped confirm the suspect's real identity.

The CEDRIC computer system was also used by Scotland Yard, so the moment a target was flagged it would show to both agencies, thereby preventing them from chasing the same suspect.

Now we had tailed our target to central London. What his purpose here was we didn't know. He could've been doing some early Christmas shopping, or he could be meeting an important contact. We had to be prepared.

Suddenly there was activity ahead. A bus had pulled out and was in-between Tango One and our eyeball. I caught sight of a black car turning right at the fork ahead.

The voice of Trevor Jardine, the case officer, came over the radio: 'Tango One has turned left to South Kensington Tube. Repeat. Tango One has turned left …'

'No!' I said, instinctively. Open radios connected each car. 'Correction. Tango One has turned right towards the Albert Hall.'

Bruce swung right and for a moment my heart was in my mouth. What if I had called that wrong?

But there it was. The black Merc. I looked round. Trevor's car had turned left. We were now the eyeball. Bruce radioed in to give everyone an update.

We tailed the suspect to Knightsbridge, feeling a slight twinge of panic as he appeared to double back on himself. Had we been spotted? No, it seemed as though he was just looking for a place to park. We watched him come to a halt. One of the other teams jumped out and followed on foot so we wouldn't show out. They tailed him to a restaurant. The teams had to swap again so another senior officer, Jack Burns, told me to join him.

It was a packed boutique restaurant opposite Harrods. We managed to get a table, but not as close as we'd have liked. Tango One, a stocky, balding character, was sitting with a burly man with a large, droopy moustache. As we tried to listen in to their conversation – nearly impossible due to the chatter of other diners – Jack wrote descriptions on the menu, noting the time and highlighting anything that might be significant.

We waited until they left, knowing that another team was waiting to pick them up outside. Meanwhile, we spoke to the waiters and explained we were Customs officers. Jack produced a handkerchief and carefully picked up the glasses the suspects had drunk from.

'We'll be able to test these for fingerprints,' he said.

I recognised the tradecraft. One of the first things I had done as a recruit was attend a Basic Intelligence Training, or BITs, course, which taught me the importance of making contemporaneous notes, preferably on a menu, or napkin, to put you at a particular place and time. And if there's an opportunity to seize evidence, take it. Over a month-long course at New Fetter Lane, we learned the theory of the laws we were enforcing, how to gather evidence, how to conduct an interview with a suspect and what we needed to have any chance of getting a case past a jury. We also had to write a report on a case of VAT fraud. But that wasn't all. We were also told the secrets of foot surveillance. It was straight out of *The French Connection*. If you've got the target in front, you have three Customs officers following. If he turns left, the person behind, who has eyeball, walks on and the next person behind turns left and continues to follow him, and so on. Across the road is a fourth officer, always staying ahead of the target. If he pops into a shop the guy across will see. Another situation we were prepared for was being able to successfully follow someone who had landed at Heathrow into the city centre.

We also learned self-defence – a handy skill, given at some stage we might be called upon to arrest someone who doesn't want to be detained. In theory, I now knew how to tackle someone if they came at me with a knife, or how to drag someone to the floor.

When we left the restaurant, we learned Tango One had gone back to his car, while the other man had jumped into a black cab.

'Are we not following it?' I said.

'No need,' Trevor said. 'Stand down.'

As we headed back to the office for a debrief, I felt buoyant. I'd stopped us losing the target and making a mess of an international job. All the team had been out and I'd shown good observation skills. It felt like a result.

Back at the office I nipped into the toilets, and Bruce followed me in.

'Don't ever do that again.'

I turned, stunned. 'What?'

'You don't counter-command a senior investigator. Ever.'

I know I was only new, but I had never seen him like this. 'But …'

The door swung shut behind him. All that lingered was a whiff of stale cigarettes. Any buzz I felt had well and truly evaporated. I just stood there, numb. Had Trevor complained to him? Why was nothing said while we were on the job? And then I understood. It wasn't about the job. It was the culture. I was young, I was new. I had to do what I was told. Don't think, don't ask questions. This was a whole different ball game. It was a level up from any other Customs department I'd been in. The hierarchy existed for a reason.

I understood, but ultimately the senior officer had got it wrong, and I had got it right. I was crestfallen. I went home deflated. What did this mean for the rest of my probation?

The next day when I went into the office, nothing more was said about my insubordination. Instead, the chat was about the progress made on the case. A call from Walt to the cab company had revealed they kept a record of their hires and they disclosed that their driver had dropped the moustachioed man to a street in Dulwich Village, south London.

Trevor checked the inhabitants of the whole of the road on the electoral roll. He put the names through CEDRIC and got a hit. At a house in the same street was a boat captain, a suspected major drug trafficker. We had the name of his contact. The operation was a success.

The Mounties were happy. In our report to them, however, I bet it failed to mention how close the case officer came to blowing it.

| | |

In the days after I was still smarting from the bollocking from Bruce. It was the last thing I needed. I'd already had a rocky start to my career in the ID when the senior investigators realised I couldn't drive. I'd only been in the office for two days when it came to light, and I'd still been marvelling at our incredible surroundings. Unlike the rest of the ID, which was based at

New Fetter Lane, our team was the first to be based at Custom House, the imposing Grade I listed building on Lower Thames Street. While the current building dated back to 1813, there had been a Customs building, in some form, at the site since the 12th century, well located to collect duty on imported goods as boats sailed up the Thames.

I was fascinated by its history. It's where Geoffrey Chaucer, poet and author of *The Canterbury Tales*, used to work as a customs comptroller for twelve years from 1374. The building's majestic Long Room was said to have been the second-highest unsupported ceiling in Europe after the Sistine Chapel.

In 1987 it belonged to the London Collection. When Customs formed the new money laundering teams they didn't have room for us in the main investigation building. The move caused some friction with the local staff because suddenly they were working alongside national division staff on the same pay grade who were earning nearly £10,000 a year more, thinking they're the God squad, wearing leather jackets to work and taking home Golf GTI surveillance cars.

Next door to Custom House was the Queen's Warehouse, where seized goods were stored. From the pungent aroma that wafted from its direction, smelling strangely like a box of After Eight mints, it wasn't hard to deduce that there were probably hundreds of kilograms of cannabis in there. It was an ever-present reminder of the scale of the operation I had joined.

|||

HM Customs Investigation Division was then divided into different sections, 'A', 'B', 'C', 'D', etc., dealing with specific areas, like strategic exports, alcohol and tobacco, textiles and VAT and commercial fraud.

Drugs fell under the prefix 'I' for India. Within India were several teams called Drugs A, B, C, D etc., all the way through the alphabet, dealing with very specific issues. Drugs B and C dealt with cannabis smugglers, F dealt with heroin smuggled by White British people, G was concerned with Asian heroin traffickers. Drugs L was Turkish heroin gangs, a problem so specific it merited its own team, who spent most of its time in Haringey, while Drugs R and S investigated cocaine importers. Drugs T looked at synthetic drugs, like LSD, MDMA and ecstasy, which were becoming increasing popular on the street. The drugs teams were grouped into branches, each with its own Assistant Chief Investigations Officer (ACIO) in charge. Branch One was cannabis, so took in Drugs B, C, D, J and K; Branch Two was heroin, which meant G, F, N, O and P; Branch Three was cocaine, so Drugs R, S and T, and so on.

The Investigation Division was a thousand-people strong, from a total Customs staff of more than 25,000. Half of the ID were investigators and half support staff, split between offices in London, Birmingham, Leeds, Manchester, Bristol and Glasgow.

There was no doubt the ID was the elite and when Customs formed the new Drug Financial Investigation Branch 16 (DFIB) as part of 'India', to enforce the new anti-money laundering legislation it was clear they had hired the best of the best to ensure the teams' success.

In the new branch four anti-money laundering teams were created. We were DFIB1 and came under the banner 'Drugs U' for Uniform, because not only did we deal with money launderers, we also helped the operational drugs teams.

Each team member was given a callsign. Mine was 'India Uniform Nine', as I was the ninth member to be recruited.

Teams DFIB2 and DFIB3 dealt with the seizure of assets,

while DFIB4 was a dedicated surveillance team. In charge of these four teams was the ACIO Geoff Heslop, a careerist civil servant who, although had been operational, had not been on the frontline for some time.

Each DFIB team had a Senior Investigating Officer (SIO). The operational boss of my team, DFIB1, was Walt Smith. He was a diminutive veteran of the old Water Guard, which predated the Customs Border Agency and, being a Londoner, had spent most of his career at Heathrow. Below the SIO, on each team, were up to six senior investigators.

We had Bruce Letheran, the taciturn, tall and slender Cornishman who pulled me up for correcting and countercommanding Trevor, had served on an anti-cannabis team for years. Vastly experienced, he was also very intelligent. Every morning since I had started, almost without fail, he had completed *The Times* crossword before beginning his work.

Then there was Henry Black, who was thought of as the best intelligence officer in the division. He had worked on the frontline for years, where he bugged suspect's telephones, working on some huge, high-profile cases throughout his career. If there was something to know, he knew it. His nickname was 'Secret Squirrel', and everything was on a need-to-know basis. He locked his drawers and even ate his biscuits on a need-to-know basis. He would open his drawer, sneak a biscuit, put it in his mouth and close it again, hoping that no one saw what he was up to. That said, he had been welcoming to me and Colin Roberts, the other young, inexperienced recruit, telling us stories of some of his big cases, like that of a famous entrepreneur who had been convicted of tax fraud.

'Of course,' Henry said, 'the guy was also one of Britain's top cocaine smugglers. That was why he was being investigated.

In the end it was easier to do him for the fraud. We also put a stop to Thatcher giving him a gong.'

Henry had a withering view of any businessperson who'd suddenly done well, or come into money, a view no doubt formed over years working on such cases. 'Nobody gets rich quick,' he said. 'There are no overnight success stories. Anyone who's suddenly made it is at it. They must have broken the law. They're on the fiddle somehow. It's our job to find out what they've done.'

Henry had worked on another team in the past – where he'd earned his reputation – but I wasn't told where. He just referred to it as 'the other office'. It wasn't with the other teams in New Fetter Lane but had its own separate set-up over in Victoria.

Jack Burns was another senior officer but, unlike the others, was a posh, public school-educated chap. When he found out I was from Sheffield he told me how he had worked on a Customs smuggling team that, for once, was not concerned with drugs.

They had been tasked with investigating several large oil companies, during the time of the miners' strike, three years earlier. They had hired a helicopter to go round the mines, like Orgreave Colliery and other coke plants, to see if there were big stockpiles of coal, as the Tories were claiming.

Prime Minister Margaret Thatcher, then under huge pressure to reverse her decision to close collieries, said the coal board was sitting on huge reserves of coal. Jack flew round dozens of pits and saw no stockpiles of coal. The miners, Jack said, were on the verge of winning the strike.

However, at the same time, Thatcher had the oil companies – seizing the moment – refusing to pay excise duties. They threatened to turn the pipes off unless she granted them a tax holiday. Without oil and coal, the country would grind to a halt and Thatcher would be finished. Even though the Treasury missed out on millions from oil duties, the producers got their way.

Like most in Sheffield, I was a huge supporter of the miners and to find out they had been days away from winning, was simply staggering. I had a sick feeling in my stomach, but at the same time it was an eye-opening reminder of the reach of Her Majesty's Customs. They knew everything about everyone.

Our other senior officer, Gary Wright, was based at New Scotland Yard. The Metropolitan Police had also set up a financial unit at the same time as Customs and they received tip offs from the banks. Every day they received around 30 forms about someone suspicious paying in large amounts of cash. If there was any hint of foreign transactions involved they passed it on to Gary.

Another key member of the team was senior officer Steve Berry, one of the cleverest people I'd ever met, and very laid back. He was from Nottingham but started in Croydon VAT office and we had a lot in common. He was as obsessed with Nottingham Forest as I was with Sheffield Wednesday.

From initial impressions, the team was a good blend of experience and youthful enthusiasm. I had only been with them a matter of weeks when the scale of the organisation and the reach of the new legislation became apparent.

Drugs D – the Deltas – was looking into a massive cannabis smuggling operation. They were a referred team, which meant the bulk of their jobs came from airports and docks. UK Customs had only recently signed a cooperation agreement with our counterparts in the Soviet Union and they had discovered three-and-a-half tonnes of cannabis hidden in a liquorice consignment, which had originated in Afghanistan and was on its way to Tilbury Docks in Essex. The Deltas asked the Russians to let the drugs run so they could see who claimed it on arrival. The recipients were some heavy London criminals, including a major drug trafficker called Jimmy Rose.

Independently, some large cash deposits made in Kent by self-employed insurance agent Andrew George had aroused suspicion within the bank with whom he'd opened a business account. They didn't believe the vast amounts of cash – one deposit alone was for over £250,000 – could have been generated by George's own small business. DFIB2 began investigating and, between them and the Deltas, they suspected George was moving cash on behalf of the cannabis smugglers, who were thought to be behind at least three other importations. George was using the cash to buy insurance bonds for some suspicious clients, including Rose.

When the time came to arrest the gang, the Deltas and DFIB2 requested help from throughout the ID. Jack Burns told me to join him to pick up George, the money launderer.

This was the moment I had been waiting for – my first knock.

We were down at George's house – a nondescript middle-class house in a commuter village south of London – before dawn.

At the briefing in the New Fetter Lane offices the day before, around 80 of us had listened to case officer James Graham issue his instructions. Our job was simply to arrest the insurance agent, while officers from DFIB2 would conduct the search to seize any assets. At various other addresses in the London area, other ID investigators waited for the nod to pounce on the drug villains.

My nerves were tingling. This was why I had wanted to join the investigators.

I heard James's SIO, a large Mancunian called Derek Henderson, come over the radio.

'Have you got the paper?' he said.

I shot a quizzical look at Jack.

'The search warrant,' he said.

I nodded. I hadn't a clue.

'Yes,' James replied.

Henderson then asked Alpha over the air to confirm. I'd never heard of this outfit, nor had they been at the briefing or on the operational sheet.

'Confirmed.'

'Right,' Derek said. 'Knock it!'

'This is it,' Jack said, 'let's go!'

We jumped out of the car and banged on the door.

George appeared, looking like he was about to go to work. He was a slim guy, in his mid-30s with curly black hair, like the comedian Bobby Ball.

Jack flashed his badge and told him why we were there. The colour drained from George's face. He didn't put up much resistance as we arrested him and took him to a local police station to begin the formal interview. By then he'd regained his composure and tried to play it down, insinuating that he had no idea of the money's origins, he just did what he was asked and invested it.

I sat and listened as Jack put all the key allegations to him. When the interview was over, we turned over all the tapes to Peter Lyle, who was handling the money laundering prosecution side of things.

The operation was a huge success. Rose wasn't arrested on the same day but was caught hiding in a caravan several months later over in the west of England. As the case progressed, it emerged that his organisation had imported three consignments of four tonnes each, from India.

George was alleged to have handled at least £1.5 million over a two-year period. When the cases came to court, Rose was jailed for twelve years and served with a £2.3 million confiscation order, although this was reduced to ten years and £1.4 million on appeal. George was jailed for a staggering nine years for money laundering, showing the power of the new legislation.

Eighteen months later we paid him a visit in prison, with an offer to reduce his sentence if he cooperated with us. We even had the power to set him free. By then he was a shadow of the man we'd detained. He looked like shit. He wasn't remotely interested in helping us.

'I cannot tell you the depravity in this place,' he said. 'You can hire a hitman in here for a couple of grand.'

The message was clear – if he talked, he'd be dead in no time.

I was thrilled to experience my first knock and arrest – but it demonstrated how much I had to learn. I had other issues to contend with too. For one, there was the small matter of my inability to drive. Walt wasn't happy, leaving me in no doubt that I wouldn't have got the job had they known. I wanted to create the right impression, so readily agreed when they asked me to sit an intensive course. I crammed in five lessons a week and passed my test in no time. My first car was a £6,000 Ford Escort Bonus, handy for driving home to Sheffield on the weekend. The team did have use of several departmental cars, but these were nearly all booked out by senior members who were allowed to take them home, providing they had out-of-office inquiries to make last thing at night or first thing in the morning, which, curiously, they seemed to have quite regularly. At some point in the future, if I passed my probation, there was a police advanced driving course to attend, which would prove invaluable on surveillance jobs.

||||

Surveillance and investigating was, however, only part of the job. A key role for DFIB1 was liaising with banks and other financial institutions, who were frankly terrified of the new legislation now there were potential prison sentences if they were caught moving money suspected to have come from drug smuggling.

The legislation was unusual because it stated you must not assist somebody to retain their assets if you know or *suspect* that they are the proceeds from drug trafficking. This was the first time that suspicion of a crime had been inserted. Before then, it was only knowledge of a crime that mattered. Now banks didn't have to *know* their customer was a drug trafficker, they just had to suspect it. It was a big thing for the institutions. Another key element was that we could transfer suspicion, so if we rang the bank up and told them we were looking at a particular person, they immediately made a note in their internal files that the individual was suspected of drug trafficking so they shouldn't assist them.

It worked both ways. If they were suspicious about someone they could make a disclosure to basically cover themselves of any culpability. All they had to do was fill a form in and send it to Scotland Yard to protect themselves from prosecution.

Not surprisingly, the police – who had also formed their own anti-money laundering teams – were inundated with disclosures. They were all put into the computer. Often, if it was just an isolated suspicion, and they weren't acted upon, but if we received a disclosure about a known target, or the same name appeared more than once, we started enquiries.

We split the institutions between us, made contacts and forged links so we could have better cooperation. If we had a target and we wanted to know how much they had in a UK bank account we could go to the banks and they would tell us. If we wanted to monitor someone's credit card transactions, they would help us. This was on the understanding it was purely to be used for intelligence. If we wanted it for evidence we had to get a court order.

The best contacts were with the big banks, like NatWest and Barclays, as these would bear more fruit, but we had good relationships with the credit card companies and building societies like Abbey and Bradford and Bingley. Some of the banks took the new legislation seriously enough to employ ex-cops to keep them right. I travelled to Merseyside to establish a connection with Giro Bank, which was based there. Every institution was contacted, even the London offices of places like the Bank of Baroda and the State Bank of India, or Habib Bank of Pakistan and the Iranian Bank Melli. We kept index cards for each institution and updated them with contacts made.

Interestingly, when I looked through the index one day, I saw that *nearly* every institution had been contacted. One card said no approach should be made. It was an international bank of Pakistani origin with its headquarters now in London ... the Bank of Credit and Commerce International.

CHAPTER 4

�111111111111111111111111111111111111

The other office

I t was hard not to get distracted. The longer you trained your eyes on a door the more they were inclined to wander.

It was the one thing they didn't teach you on the BITs course – how to deal with the boredom of a stakeout. We had been outside the same address, on and off, for days, and I was losing the will to live. At least it wasn't the worst place to hang out. We were back in Knightsbridge, clearly a sought-after area for international drug smugglers, just around the corner from Harrods.

My companion once again was Bruce, and most of our time together in the car passed in silence. It was two months on from his bollocking, and I hadn't knowingly given him further cause to be annoyed. Whether he was still unhappy with me, it was hard to tell. He didn't say as much, but Bruce didn't give much away. And I'd learnt my lesson. Shut up, speak when spoken to, stay alert. This was a big case; Bruce was in charge. I would do what I was told.

The US Drug Enforcement Administration (DEA) had tasked us. They were on the trail of two brothers, Bill and Chris Shaffer, who were part of a massive criminal conspiracy responsible for bringing tonnes of south-east Asian marijuana and Thai sticks – whole-bud cannabis cigars, wrapped in leaves – into America, earning them hundreds of millions of dollars.

Bill Shaffer's public image was as an international playboy, living the dream as he travelled the world, visiting only the most glamorous cities, staying in the best hotels, eating at the finest restaurants, hanging out with the A-listers at exclusive parties and befriending some of show business's hottest actresses. To the jet-set he must have looked like any other self-made millionaire. But what his newfound celebrity friends didn't know was that it was all a lie.

The Shaffers were part of a network that the DEA suspected were some of the biggest importers of cannabis to the USA. Interpol referred to the network as The Ring and had uncovered multiple layers to the vast criminal organisation that stretched from Britain to America and from Thailand to Australia. Many of the Shaffers' cohorts were just like them; playboys and former hippies who latterly got their kicks from flying helicopters or racing powerboats. Some were ex-military special forces, so brought a wealth of knowledge to help with the logistics of such a large-scale international operation.

Bill Shaffer was an experienced diver and had an ingenious front company, offering a specialist service salvaging porcelain from shipwrecks at the bottom of the South China Sea. Ming vases provided the perfect cover answer as to why he had so many boating contacts, and why he had to make regular trips to that part of the world. It also explained the type of gear in which it would be easy to hide contraband. By the time the DEA contacted us they had been on his tail for years.

The Ring was so successful it was said the Shaffers had even bought their own island in the Caribbean, a very clever move. Owning an island meant they could operate an exclusion zone around it. It was said they'd built underwater tanks to store the gear. Whatever they had left over, the DEA had reasons to suspect it was being laundered in the UK. The source of the monies used to buy the £3-million Knightsbridge townhouse we were watching was not untraceable.

Bruce was the case officer for our operation and, so far, our inquiries had established that Bill Shaffer regularly rang a known British ship's captain and smuggler on the Essex coast. We liaised with the local police there and they were able to provide valuable intelligence on the captain – suspected criminal activity, boat yards he visited and vessels he had bought and renovated to sell on. The DEA were delighted. They'd thought Shaffer was only here to move money but from our intelligence it seemed far bigger than that. They instructed us to follow Shaffer and try to glean some more information.

That was what brought us to Knightsbridge. What gave this operation some added intrigue was the suggestion that Shaffer lived in this townhouse with his glamorous TV-actress girlfriend, Cherie Lunghi. She was making a name for herself, having just starred alongside Robert De Niro in a period drama that had received some acclaim. There was no suggestion she knew anything about his criminal enterprise, and whether they were still in a relationship was debatable, as so far we hadn't seen them together.

In fact, we hadn't seen much at all, which is the time when complacency sets in. Just when you think your targets aren't at home is the moment your attention is distracted by some passers-by, and precisely when your quarry nips out and jumps into a waiting taxi. That's why it was important to stay vigilant.

We were sitting a few doors away from the townhouse, so as not to arouse suspicion, not from the target house at least. You always run the risk that a neighbour might take exception to two men sitting in a car outside their home for hours on end. That's why we needed to be alert to any changes around us. Which was why my gaze shifted briefly at the sight of two people coming out of a door just yards away from our car. I did a double take. Was that who I thought it was?

It was an actress, not the one we were expecting to see, but an altogether much bigger name. Shirley MacLaine, Oscar-winning star of *Terms of Endearment*, sister of Warren Beatty and genuine Hollywood legend, had just walked out of a house. I would have recognised her anywhere. I watched *The Apartment* nearly every Christmas. And who was with her? The political broadcaster and journalist Robin Day. I have always wondered if this was the senior Labour politician she discusses in her memoirs.

I pointed it out to Bruce. 'Fuck me, you're right.'

They looked very much like a couple. It wasn't our place to judge or make comment. For all I knew they were both single and might have been friends for years, It was just odd seeing two very famous faces together, while we were sitting looking for someone else. I imagined some of the tabloid showbiz writers would have liked the scoop.

They seemed oblivious to our presence and in seconds they were out of sight. My focus went back to the door in question, but suddenly something else caught my eye. A man, standing at a bus stop, suddenly keeled over. Bloody hell!

I looked at Bruce. His hand was already on the key in the ignition. He paused, perhaps to make sure there were people running to the man's aid, and that we weren't the only witnesses to his health emergency. As we pulled away, several passers-by and residents were helping him.

As callous as it sounds, we couldn't get involved. We weren't meant to be there. It was an international surveillance operation.

We couldn't do anything that might compromise it, and so we left, and waited until an ambulance arrived to take the unfortunate man to hospital before resuming our watch.

Sitting with Bruce for hours at a time didn't bring us closer together. That wasn't his personality. He was very private and, I imagined, quite modest. While some other senior investigators loved to share their war stories, Bruce was more discreet, which was a pity as I'm sure he could have shared some fascinating experiences. As it was, we just had to tolerate each other's company for as long as it took.

| | |

When I first joined the Uniforms, the resources at our disposal impressed me, but it was nothing to what the intelligence services could call upon. On an operation that only consisted of our team we could call upon four cars and often a motorbike if we needed to tail someone through central London. Steve Berry told me that when MI5 followed a target, they used 25 vehicles, with two people in each. I realised then that we were doing it on the cheap.

It didn't help that the company cars at our disposal were limited. We had a souped-up Mercedes, but nobody could get it off the boss Geoff Heslop. My favourite was the black Volkswagen Golf GTI, but I rarely got my hands on it. For all the fuss Walt made about me not being able to drive, since I passed my test, I was hardly ever behind the wheel. The senior officers always wanted to drive. I suspected this was because, if it rained, they wouldn't be the ones required to jump out and continue the follow on foot.

For the next few weeks, the Shaffer case took up most of my time. I made trips to Essex to liaise with the police there, and a friendly detective kept me informed on any developments regarding the ship's captain. Bill Shaffer called him sometimes from his home phone. I spent some time watching the captain's address and then coming back to London to continue the surveillance on Shaffer.

We soon suspected he was moving millions through London to Switzerland. We hadn't yet established how, but it was known millions of dollars of dirty cash was being flown to Heathrow by courier companies. It was easy. You could pay a courier company and send it to yourself. Millions of dollars in notes were found at the airport, virtually spilling out of boxes, fairly regularly. We then believed he was moving the money on by renting a plane and flying out of the former RAF base at Cardington, in Bedfordshire.

It was a time-consuming operation, but I enjoyed being part of something so big. I just concentrated on doing the best job I could and showing I could add value to the team. By the end of March 1988, I was conscious that I had been there for six months, and my probation was coming to an end. Just when I was wondering how I would hear if I was staying on, Heslop summoned me to his office.

He got straight to the point. 'You've passed your probation. You're here, good luck.'

'Thank you.'

'Now you're here with us for the long term, there's a secret I can let you in on,' he said.

What could he mean? Was there an executive toilet I'd now get a key for? A little-known tip on how to get the GTI more often? My mind raced at the possibilities.

'We have a secret unit only a few teams know about and are able to call upon,' he said, leaning over his desk conspiratorially.

I nodded.

'It's called Alpha. They operate from a separate office, they are our secret weapon against the smugglers and there's a very good reason we keep it hushed up.'

'They can intercept phone calls,' he went on, 'but don't tell anyone outside of here about it. We don't want the people we're targeting to get wind of it.'

Of course, 'the other office' I'd heard Henry talk about, and the outfit on the Russian job.

I was desperate to know more, but Heslop was clearly done.

'Once the others know you've been told, they can talk to you more about it.'

I shook his hand and left the office, relieved that I had passed my probation and intrigued to learn more about this mysterious 'other office'.

Now it made sense. Henry knew everybody and everything and was so highly regarded he had obviously served on Alpha for years. It was to him I went for more information.

He told me Alpha was set up in the early eighties and back then was staffed by about a dozen senior officers, who were at the equivalent level of detective inspector in the Criminal Investigation Department. These twelve officers were split into A and B shifts, covering 6am to 10pm, seven days a week, 365 days a year. Each operation had two case officers, one from each of the shifts, so there was always someone with full knowledge of the case on duty. Soon, however, it turned into a 24-hour operation.

The advantage Alpha had over the police and intelligence services was that they always listened 'live' to phone calls. While the police were generally reactive, acting after listening to inter-cept recordings, Alpha could act immediately, tasking officers to witness meetings, shadow suspects or follow targets anywhere, apprehend villains or move if they believed a smuggling operation was going down right at that moment.

From its conception, Alpha handpicked the best of the best. There was no interview. Officers were 'invited' to join. People like Henry Black were expected to serve three years, and their time there always guaranteed them a senior management role once they'd completed their stint. Henry ended up spending ten years there – which shows how good he was.

But Alpha became a victim of its own success – and the rapid evolution of technology. It produced such great results, but it was at the mercy of an increasing workload. Second landlines and the availability of mobile phones meant more calls to monitor. Officers had to stay on longer and when they were allowed to move there was no longer the guaranteed promotion, which explained why someone like Henry was still at senior level.

And, while it was an exceptional tool in the fight against crime, it wasn't perfect. The intelligence couldn't be used as evidence in court and, operationally, its results could be frustrating. Criminals rarely used their real full names over the phone and routinely used nicknames or callsigns. Instructions were given in code, so it was down to the officers on the ground to make sense of what was said. Invariably Customs investigators regularly received reports littered with references to 'UKM' and 'UKF', meaning unknown males and females.

Later that day, Jack took me across to the Drugs G team – 'Golf' – to assist with a job they were doing. Each drug team had a link officer on DFIB1 and Jack was the Golfs' go-to man. They wanted a financial check done with Barclays on a target. While we were there a phone rang, unanswered, on an empty desk. I answered it.

'Get Golf One to 10/9 me,' a voice said. It rung off.

Phone who? I wondered.

'Don't ever answer that!' Jack said. 'No one can touch that but the SIO.

'That's the "bat phone" – the direct line to Alpha,' he added, perhaps seeing the bemusement on my face. 'Every drugs team has one, except us. We're not set up yet. Henry's our contact with them.'

Okay, I thought, they are definitely serious about how hush-hush this secret unit had to be.

When we got back to the office Steve Berry greeted me.

'I hear you passed your probation, congratulations.'

I was about to thank him and say how much I was looking forward to getting stuck into more cases, when he cut me off.

'It was touch and go whether you'd be kept on.'

'What?!'

'At the end of your probation, Bruce said to Heslop, "Send him back." I said, "You are fucking crazy, he's young, he's raw, he's Yorkshire, but he's keen and intelligent. Plus, we can't afford to send him back because we don't have the staff."'

Talk about being brought back down to earth with a crash. I had no idea I was that close to being on my way back to Sheffield. Thanks to Steve, they kept me on. I had no reason to doubt him. He was so well-regarded no one would have said a word against him.

Bruce never said anything to me about the decision, but a few days later he suggested we go to Essex together for a few days, to find out the latest on Shaffer's boatman. We spent two days on the coast but, while there were no dramas, there was no real breakthrough in our relationship. We still didn't know each other. We had nothing in common. We weren't antagonistic, there was just no bond there.

They might not be sending me back to the provinces, but I still had a lot to learn.

CHAPTER 5

||||||||||||||||||||||||||||||||||||||||||

Following the money

The job sounded intriguing.

The Golfs – Drugs G – were looking into a heroin-smuggling operation from India. The drugs teams were either referred teams or targeted teams. Referred teams worked on cases were, for example, Customs at a port or airport rang up and said they'd just seized ten kilos of cocaine. If the referred case was big enough, or had a sensitive or international connection that could be developed, then the relevant ID drugs team would take it on. If they deemed it too small, they would leave it to the local Collection Investigation Unit (CIU).

Target teams worked solely with Alpha. They were effectively Alpha's operational footmen, so were always working off telephone intercepts. The Golfs were a target team. They were investigating a group of drug importers that had links to Southall, an area of west London known as little Punjab, so strong were its South Asian connections.

During Alpha's monitoring of the targets' telephones, one name kept coming up in conversations – that of an Asian travel agent in Wembley. He spoke to the smack smugglers regularly on the blower, in code. Was he the money launderer of profits here? Or remitting cash to pay for product? Alpha suspected both, so the Golfs got in touch with Jack Burns to see if we could check out his financial status. Jack passed it to me. My first case with Alpha.

'Don't get too excited,' Jack said. 'Sounds like a *hawala* job.'

'A what?'

'*Hawala*. Look it up. Will probably mean it's a dead end. Which is why a junior's getting it,' he said, laughing.

I did as Jack suggested and dug out an academic report.

Dating back to the 8th century in India, *hawala* was an ancient system of transferring money great distances. There are variations around the world. In Persia, it was known as *havaleh*, while in Somalia it went by the name of *xawala*. Another similar system, which also originated in India, is *hundi*, where remittance slips were issued in place of cash.

Hawala was designed for Indian and Arabic traders operating along the Silk Road network of routes connecting China with the Indian subcontinent, Asia, Arabia and the Horn of Africa, primarily as a means of protection from robbery, but it was so effective it remained popular centuries later. In the wake of the UK's new stringent anti-money laundering legislation, it was proving to be a near fool-proof way around it.

Reading the report, I was amazed at the simplicity of the system. A customer could be anyone with money to transfer. It wasn't limited to drug smuggling – it bypassed exchange controls, for example – but, obviously, contraband transactions had more reason to be kept discreet. A customer in London could approach a *hawala* broker, and give them the sum of money they want to be transferred. Usually, this would be to a customer in another city, or continent. In addition to the money, he would also give the broker – or *hawaladar* – a password needed to receive the money at the other end. The *hawaladar* calls a broker in the recipient's city and supplies the password.

The intended recipient just needs to approach the broker in his home city, give the right password and the funds will be handed over. Obviously, at some point, the cash must be transferred between the *hawala* brokers, or reconciled in some way, but the beauty of it is that it is record free. There is no paper trail.

Unlike banks, you don't need an account, a passport or ID number to transfer huge sums. *Hawala* traders don't have any hidden charges such as a delivery and transfer fees, don't require expensive bankers' drafts and they don't have to wait on couriers or several days clearance. They often charge a small commission – usually no more than 5 per cent – but they offer more favourable rates of exchange than banks and, most importantly, there are no questions asked. They don't care where the money has come from.

It was astonishing that such a system could function, essentially based on trust, but, very occasionally, evidence of it existed in bank accounts – suggesting the figures involved were staggering.

Steve Berry had a case on behalf of an operational team concerning a pharmacist who owned a small chemist shop in north London. He ran a one-man-band operation, but his name kept coming up in conversations between drug traffickers. When we did a financial check and contacted NatWest, they told us he had £67 million in his bank account. Either a lot of people got headaches and colds in Finchley, or he had a lucrative sideline business. That was an exceptional situation, we discovered. The problem with *hawala*, from our perspective, was that nothing touched the formal balance. It was all unregulated and virtually untraceable.

Although there was reasonable intelligence on *hawala*, what didn't seem to be known was how the money was moved abroad. Surely at some point the cash had to be reconciled?

Regarding the travel agent, before deciding if it was a *hawala* case, the main question was whether he was a player in the smuggling operation or an innocent whose name just happened to come up. In Alpha's report there was nothing conclusive. They heard our target saying things like, 'give me the money' or 'I'll take it to your cousin', but that wasn't strong enough evidence and there were no clues as to who the recipient was. No one had done any physical surveillance on him yet.

I put his details into CEDRIC to signify that he was our target and began a thorough investigation into his work and home addresses, background and movements. First, I checked out the travel agency. In Wembley or Southall, where there were high populations of ethnic minorities, there was no point attempting static surveillance. We would show out in no time. Brief street surveillance, where my fellow junior officer and I watched from a parked car, established he worked at the shop from Monday to Saturday. We then 'housed' him, meaning we scoped out his home address – outside London, in High Wycombe – from background checks, and then confirmed it by late-night and early-morning drive-bys. Although it was a quiet, residential area we had more success here than at the agency.

I decided we needed to follow him on a Sunday, my theory being that this might be the day he did his 'other' business, perhaps believing that he was less likely to be bothered by British officialdom, who either wouldn't want to or couldn't afford to work weekends.

At the ID, we weren't paid overtime, but got a double-time credit to work on Sundays and for this one I got the whole team out. If we were going to do it, we needed to do it properly. It also had to be for more than five hours, as this generated a daily expense allowance. No one worked less.

Shortly before midday the travel agent left his house, carrying a holdall, got in his car, and headed south down the A404 towards the M25. We had four cars in pursuit, so were able to change formation, confident that we weren't showing out. He headed towards Heathrow Airport but, instead of aiming for one of the terminals, he turned off at the Posthouse Hotel. I followed him on foot as he entered the hotel and watched as he bypassed reception and headed straight upstairs to one of the rooms. He knew exactly where he was going.

I tailed him to the fifth floor and watched as he knocked on the door of a room and was quickly let in. Clearly someone had been expecting him.

I went down to security and showed my ID. Customs investigators carried both an identity card and gold badge, designed to be worn on an outside pocket, which we would do whenever we were on a raid. The security chief checked the records and said the entire fifth floor was block-booked by Air India, for its cabin crew.

This was fascinating. Were Air India unwitting couriers in the *hawala* system? It looked that way. We were fortunate that the airline booked its staff into a big, corporate hotel. Already I'd seen, with the banks, how institutions were willing to help us if we suspected criminal activity going on. If our travel agent had led us to a small, family-run hotel, we would not have been so lucky.

We kept eyeball on the room and our target reappeared after a few minutes, still carrying his doctor's bag. Some of the team followed him home, while the rest continued our watch, and it was early the following morning when an Air India stewardess left the room, with a small suitcase and carry-on baggage.

We primed the team at Heathrow Customs, so they were ready to covertly scan the stewardess's suitcase when she arrived for her flight to Delhi. Cabin crews are generally subjected to less constraints than regular travellers, so we didn't want to arouse any suspicion. We didn't stop her or cause a scene but, once her bag was with security, our Customs colleagues photographed the contents. There were thousands and thousands of pounds inside. They asked us what we wanted to do. We made the decision to let it run.

While the Golfs were still working on the case there was nothing to be gained from detaining an air stewardess and quizzing her about the source of the cash. The operation would have been blown. The anti-money laundering legislation then was only for drug money but, *hawala* cash could be proceeds of drugs or tax fraud or currency smuggling. Proving the money in that consignment was proceeds of narcotics was impossible without one of two things; an informant who was prepared to give evidence or an undercover officer.

It had been an extremely valuable exercise. For the first time we had shown one method used by *hawaladars* to get their money from Britain and other Western countries to India or Pakistan.

From the way *hawala* brokers advertised in magazines distributed among their communities you would think it was a legal practice. It was not. In most Asian countries, where exchange controls were then imposed, the cash should have been declared, otherwise, at the very least, it was currency smuggling.

As far as our involvement went, we had exhausted our options, but it was an eye-opener. It might not have led to any arrests but the intelligence our inquiries produced contributed to some innovative and bold moves in the future in our bid to tackle money launderers.

CHAPTER 6

|||||||||||||||||||||||||||||||||||||||

The tricks of the trade

Now that the secrets of Alpha were unlocked for me, I was able to witness the reach of this powerful tool, and the scale of the resources at Customs' disposal.

It wasn't long before we were back in a Heathrow hotel again. It was Henry's case, which invariably meant it had originated from Alpha. Their intercepts had led us to follow a potential laundry man to his room. With the help of hotel security, we booked the room next door and placed a bug in the target's room. This was my first sight of Customs' specialist technical team, as they worked away setting up our room to listen in to what was happening through the wall. The hotel management were fully on board, with room service staff helping out with access.

We took it in turns to do twelve-hour shifts, listening for any evidence of how much money was at stake and what he planned to do with it. While there wasn't much chatter from the room to do with financial transactions, Henry did report having to listen in to some interesting bedroom antics, and he admitted it was a fairly regular occurrence for him.

Like a lot of Henry jobs, I only knew basic details of the background. I might have passed my probation, but Henry still operated on a need-to-know basis, and that limited information was communicated so softly you had to strain to hear, as he moved only his bottom-left lip. The hotel bug had not produced any damning evidence, but I got the impression from Henry that there were some useful leads. As was the case with a lot of our operations, they were for intelligence-gathering, primarily, rather than to arrest someone.

He did invite me along on another job – a request from the US embassy. As we had done with the Canadian Mounties, we met with our American counterparts, who explained they were on the trail of some corrupt money men. During our meeting they introduced me to the concept of 'smurfing'.

This, I was intrigued to learn, had nothing to do with little, blue, Belgian cartoon characters, but the depositing of illegally gained money into multiple bank accounts to avoid suspicion. In an attempt to curb money laundering, any transfer or deposit of anything over $10,000 had to be declared in the States, so a lot of criminals tried to get round this by depositing $9,900 at a time into separate bank accounts.

The term 'smurf' came from gangs manufacturing synthetic drugs like methamphetamine. To avoid suspicion when acquiring large quantities of chemicals, drug producers sent several of their gang to buy smaller amounts from multiple sources, without exceeding the legal limit. Within the industry, these buyers were called 'smurfs'.

The US Customs officers explained exactly how it worked in terms of money laundering. There were three stages to smurfing: placement, layering and integration. Placement is when the money launderer, or bag man, puts the cash in a suitcase and smuggles it to another country.

According to them, London was a soft target because of our lax financial laws – even accounting for the recent legislation.

If you went down to Heathrow cargo in the eighties, dollars were virtually spilling out of UPS packages and parcels from other US courier companies. Using London was also considered another way around the $10,000 banking limit.

Layering is when illegally obtained cash is separated from its source, breaking the link to drugs or the crime that produced it. Once this happens, there is no paper trail or evidence to connect it to any crime. This could be done by a smurf transferring the funds from one bank to another, from one country to another or where the original deposit is split into smaller investments. Another option is the money could be invested into a legitimate business venture, property or high-end status purchase.

Integration is when the cash is returned to the drug smugglers, or criminals, completely laundered and stain free, from the legitimate source. If done successfully, there will be no trace to the original crime.

Unscrupulous financial institutions could help oil this process by what was known as 'cuckoo smurfing'. If a US crook wanted to transfer funds to a UK crook, they could find a willing legitimate UK businessman that needs to send the same funds to a US businessman.

The UK businessman goes to his bank in London and instructs it to send $9,000 to the US businessman's bank. The London banker, knowing the real reason for the transfer, tells the US crook to deposit $9,000 into the US businessman's bank. The London banker then transfers $9,000 from the UK businessman's account to the UK crook. The US businessman and UK businessman need never know the money was never directly transferred between them. All they're concerned with is that the debt was paid.

But the London banker could be prosecuted if caught.

Even with our anti-money laundering law, which was limited to the proceeds of drugs, the Americans believed London was wide open for smurfing and moving big amounts of money, as it was far less controlled than the States. The 'Big Bang' – Margaret Thatcher's sudden deregulation of the London financial markets in 1986 – had seen to that, prompting an increasing number of US criminals to send their money to the UK. In fact, at that time, a Japanese Bank offered £80 million to Custom House for a new City HQ. The government rejected it.

As Henry told me: 'There is only one rule in the City and that is: don't get caught.'

Hardly anyone in London's financial hub cared about the source of funds or what would be done with it. All they were interested in was their bonus and commission. Occasionally, we would go for lunch in Leadenhall Market in the City and share bars with brokers. The conversations we overheard and monitored on their new mobile phones testified to this. One colleague, Carole, was married to a mergers and acquisitions banker and their second car, a Toyota Celica, was parked on the quay at Custom House most days. Given the rest of the vehicles on show, that was like coming into work in a Ferrari back then. And she was the only one who could get the best tickets for the megastars at Wembley, like Michael Jackson. That's to take nothing away from her skills as an officer and her knowledge of the city was invaluable at times.

The main reason for our visit to the American embassy – aside from sharing their general intelligence – was to follow someone believed to be a drugs money-mover. He came into the UK on a regular flight, and rarely carried more than $1 million at a time.

For this job, Henry introduced me to the Customs' cab

– another ingenious tool in the fight against crime. It was possibly our greatest mobile surveillance weapon. To all intents and purposes, it was a regular, black, London hackney taxi. It had the yellow 'hire' light – which was never switched on, of course. Used when following a target in central London, it was a godsend. It was practically invisible. No target rumbled it. The taxi was shared between 40 or so operational teams and Alpha took priority, so it was hardly ever available, but when it was free it was invaluable. We stored it in a covert garage in Islington, where mechanics changed the registration plates on it for each new job. For central London it was amazing but, for obvious reasons, you couldn't take it out to the countryside.

The first time I saw the Customs cab used was not for an Alpha job, but another request from US Customs. Henry was, again, in charge. The Americans had specific intelligence about a money launderer flying into Heathrow. We were to follow him into the City and see where he deposited the money. Their information was accurate and we picked up the target as planned. He was carrying a bag, which Customs said contained just under $100,000. Once we entered central London, the taxi was on his tail and followed him as he headed towards the City. Unfortunately, I had to make do with being in one of the other cars. To our surprise, his cab stopped in Hammersmith and he jumped out, leaving the bag in the taxi. The £100,000 was just sitting there, while he went into a newsagent and emerged with a packet of cigarettes. We stayed on his tail until he reached a private bank on Moorgate. Funnily enough, Henry was the dedicated liaison for this merchant bank. I suspected this was just one element in a long running case and it was no coincidence Henry was the point of contact, both for the bank and for US Customs. Of course, he never confirmed this.

One of the few things Henry did say to Colin, the other junior officer, and me about foreign operations was to always try to get photographic evidence.

'Always get some good photos,' he said, 'and you may have to go abroad to give evidence in the court case. America's best,' he continued, 'as you spend two luxurious weeks waiting for the trial to begin, then they do a last-minute plea deal so the case is settled and you don't even have to give evidence live.'

Colin's ears pricked up at that. A keen photographer, some of his kit was on a par with the equipment we had at our disposal, so he was always willing to snap away if required.

|||

Since the new legislation had been introduced in the UK, several British Overseas Territories also wanted to introduce it, as for them, money laundering was an ever-increasing problem. I was about to embark on my first foreign trip, flying out to Gibraltar, Jersey, Guernsey and the Isle of Man, to fill them in on the new law and what it entailed.

Henry wanted to know how I was getting to Gib.

'Flying,' I said, slightly confused. 'There're direct flights from Heathrow.'

'Yeah, only twice a week,' he replied. I was forgetting he'd worked there during his younger days. 'And it's only two-and-a-half hours,' he said, shaking his head. 'You can't go business class unless your journey is more than three.'

'I know, but I don't really care,' I said.

'You should do it from Heathrow, but go via Spain,' he said. 'Change in Madrid. It will take four hours in total, and you'll get to fly business class, free champers, everything.'

I laughed, thinking he was joking, but he was deadly serious.

'Do it. If you don't, you'll make the rest of us look bad.'

It was a reminder of the mentality of many in the public sector.

This was summer, 1988, and Steve Berry had already been out to Gibraltar a few months earlier. He told me a story about the new chief of police there, who was a friend of his. He had been sent out there just before his retirement, no doubt expecting an easy posting so he could sit back and put his feet up before picking up his pension. This was common within the public sector, police and Customs. Just before you retired, they promoted you, because it boosted your pension, as it was based on your final salary. His first day on duty was on 6 March. He arrived to find a lot of commotion in the office.

'Much going on?' he said.

'Yes,' someone told him. 'The SAS have just liquidated three IRA terrorists down the road.'

Talk about a baptism of fire. First day on the job and he had to deal with the shooting of three people in broad daylight, the ramifications of which would run for years. The military called in the SAS because they believed the three were mounting a car bomb attack on the changing of the guard ceremony outside the governor's residence. Although they were unarmed and a car left nearby to an assembly point for the parade was found not to contain any explosives, a second car found on mainland Spain did. A later inquest on Gibraltar found the killings to be lawful.

I hoped to have a more peaceful time of it when I visited the rock.

Gibraltar had a particular problem, given that it was home to branches of UK banks, and was also so close to Morocco, a major source of dope. British smugglers had opened accounts in Gibraltar, bought the product in Morocco, sold those products in the UK, carried the cash on private flights from small southern airfields to the south of Spain, then deposited it in the UK banks on Gib. When they needed the funds to pay the Moroccans, who were only an hour away, they withdrew it from the UK banks and took it across to Tangier to pay the producers.

Before I flew out there, all the noises from the Gibraltar government were that they wanted a similar Drug Trafficking Offences Act to ours. That wouldn't take long to put in place, however I could see a major problem was going to be government corruption.

Our advice to them was to write a law that extended to the proceeds of crime, and not one limited solely to drug trafficking. We had already seen the limitations of such an act in the UK.

The Gibraltar government were not keen. Many there made a fortune from tobacco smuggling. They were happy with a law clamping down on the proceeds of drug trafficking, but nothing else. They didn't want to entertain me, basically, and it was rather a wasted trip. The border to Spain was closed at the time, so I kicked my heels hanging out with the Barbary macaques at the top of the rock, where GCHQ operated a massive spy base.

Thankfully, my arrival was greeted more favourably in the other British territories, who were more open to adopting laws with greater reach.

| | |

On my return to the UK, the jobs came in thick and fast. Howard Marks, the notorious international drug smuggler and public enemy number one was in Spain, wanted for extradition to the US to face charges there. The name didn't mean anything to me, but Henry told me the story of how this incredibly intelligent son of a Merchant Navy captain managed to rise from relatively humble beginnings in Bridgend, in industrial south Wales, to read physics at Oxford, before becoming one of the world's most successful cannabis smugglers. Henry knew of him after working on a case to try and bring him to justice in the UK.

In 1979, the Trafficante Colombian crime family, who were already importing vast quantities of cannabis into the US on freighter ships, shipped 50 tons of cannabis from Colombia to Marks and his UK associates, which was nearly enough to supply the entire British market with the drug for a year. A year later HM Customs arrested Marks after £15 million worth of cannabis originating from the Trafficante family was seized. When he was arrested, Marks was caught with a raft of incriminating evidence. Despite this, at his trial, Marks concocted a story that he was working on behalf of MI6 – where he did in fact have a mate from Oxford – and pleaded not guilty. The jury bought the tale and acquitted him on the charge of drug smuggling, but found him guilty of using false passports. The court sentenced Marks to two years in jail, but he only served five days due to time already served. Customs arrested him again for his role in an earlier 1973 smuggling operation, but his lawyers struck a deal which saw him serve just three months of a three-year sentence.

Come 1988, UK and US Customs were after him and Jack Burns asked me to provide all of Marks' UK passport applications. The aliases he'd used over the years were numerous. I filled in a request form and sent it to the passport office. They sent back twenty false applications, all in different names.

Marks was eventually extradited to the States, where he was found guilty of drug smuggling and sentenced to 25 years.

The DEA insisted he serve his sentence in the feared, federal Terre Haute prison in Indiana, perhaps to teach him a lesson. In fact, his eccentric British personality and vast intellect meant he endeared himself to the prison population and he ended up befriending a host of notorious criminals, including several Mob bosses, and he helped several inmates appeal against their convictions or sentences or further their education. He was released after serving only five years of his stretch.

||||

A big part of our job at DFIB1 was to support the operational drug teams, and so they would often ask us to ring our contacts at the banks if they were targeting an importer. Being able to establish any unusual activity in their accounts was a phenomenal source of intelligence. For instance, a credit card check on a cocaine dealer waiting for a courier to come back from Colombia could find out that he was currently staying in a hotel in Miami and had bought a ticket for a flight from Florida to Heathrow. Now you know when he's entering the country.

The more the banks got used to the legislation the greater their own checks on customers if there was unusual activity in their accounts. We heard of one bank who, when faced with a customer who wanted to deposit several thousand pounds worth in cash, asked him where the money came from.

'Smuggling coke,' he answered, quite matter-of-factly.

The bank contacted our team. We passed it on to the operational team. It turned out he wasn't lying.

Some red flags were less obvious but worth investigating. For instance, any links to destinations like Colombia were treated with suspicion.

Alpha had one such case. They asked us to check out a crime family in Essex that had been making trips to Colombia. They hadn't so far been convicted of any drug offence but one of the sons had been going on a spending spree – splashing out £20,000 a month on new clothes at posh shops in St James's and Knightsbridge. He had been known to make visits to Colombia and one of his close associates did have a conviction for a cannabis offence. We called on the same copper in Essex who had been so helpful on the Shaffer case, which was still rumbling on.

He revealed the police had been looking into the family for some time. They were a notorious bunch and were suspected of murder, extortion and other nasty crimes. So far, however, there hadn't been enough evidence to charge them with any crime. On the advice of the senior officers, I went to Southwark Crown Court and got a judge to sign a production order so we could access their bank accounts for evidence. We served the order on the bank, however, we learned through our police contact that our request had been fed back to the family. It therefore appeared we had a bent bank manager. There was no other way they could have learned about the order to access their accounts. Tipping off a criminal about an investigation was now an offence, but no one had yet been prosecuted. Bruce and I interviewed the bank manager. It would have been one of the first cases of its kind but, perhaps predictably, he denied it, probably suspecting there was no evidence. That was our last involvement with the case. As far as I was aware, it was passed to an operational drug team.

All our cases were being wrapped up or passed over to other teams. The one I was most angry about was Shaffer, which was transferred to the Met. We'd been making real progress over a number of weeks and had seen Bill Shaffer at the Knightsbridge address. As he came out of the house one day, he looked over in our direction. Bruce immediately got out of the car. Just when I thought he might be going to say something to our target, he casually went to the rear, opened the boot and pretended to look for something. Shaffer gave us no more than a cursory glance and went about his business. It was a simple but effective piece of surveillance technique.

Our friendly cop in Essex was proving to be an asset. We had got access to the Shaffer accounts with Coutts and Co., the Queen's bankers, and we had finally established his movements, confirming that he flew out of Cardington airfield in a small private plane. I was excited at how well it was going – too well, as it turned out, because clearly Scotland Yard found out about it.

They 'stroked us' – the term we used when someone stole from us. Just when I thought I'd be looking forward to a nice trip to the States to give evidence in a future trial, we were no longer on it. Clearly, the flagging system on CEDRIC could be bypassed when fame, foreign trips and promotions were at stake.

As the years passed it was frustrating to watch the case progress from afar. Bill Shaffer was eventually arrested in Germany in January 1992 and spent nine months in prison there, while his brother Chris remained a fugitive. Before he turned himself in, Chris offered to hand over more than $1 million in forfeited assets to the US government in a bid to reduce their sentences. By the time they were convicted and sentenced in Seattle, in July 1993, they were among the last of their network to appear in court. In total, the five-year investigation into their enterprise led to the convictions of 47 people.

Bill Shaffer was sentenced to thirteen-and-a-half years for two drug smuggling charges and one money laundering offence, while Chris got twelve years, for three smuggling charges and one money laundering offence. Two associates were also convicted of smuggling and money laundering offences and ordered to forfeit $450,000 between them, while another was done solely for money laundering.

It was a remarkable result – but didn't tell the full story.

Some of my senior colleagues told me the US couldn't get hold of Shaffer legally, so they waited until he made one of his trips to Switzerland and effectively kidnapped him before flying him back to the States, via Germany. It was an extraordinary case of rendition, long before the Iraq War shone a light on the practice.

It could have been another perfect case for Customs to showcase its new anti-money laundering team, but what I didn't know at the time was that our decks were being cleared for something bigger. A new case was about to land on our laps that had its origins in the forthcoming race for the White House and would have far-reaching consequences for Pablo Escobar's mighty Medellín cartel, a corrupt international bank, and would expose how the City of London helped criminal gangs move their ill-gotten gains under the nose of the Bank of England.

CHAPTER 7

Takedown

The first inkling I had that something big was coming our way was later that summer, when Bruce explained that he was privy to a case US Customs had been working on for some time. They had infiltrated a corrupt global bank, whose headquarters were here in the City of London.

'It's an undercover operation,' he said. 'They've penetrated the Colombian cartels. It's an undercover couple – a man and a woman, posing as a money launderer and his fiancée. The British connection is that they have evidence the bank in London is willingly accepting drug money. We have one, possibly two targets to investigate.'

'What's the bank?' I asked, my pulse already quickening.

'BCCI.'

The Bank of Credit and Commerce International. The one bank we didn't have a liaison with. How long had we known about this US investigation?

'Our main target is Asif Baakza, the manager of BCCI's corporate unit here in London,' Bruce said. 'The undercover officer has met him and has got him on tape. He's moved money thinking it's from drug smugglers.'

'What do you want me to do?'

'Just do all the usual background stuff. But softly, softly. Don't show out. We don't want to spook this guy until we get the word. Don't do anything that might make him spot you or recognise you. Keep it very low key and don't follow him. It's a highly sensitive, global operation.'

I nodded. 'What are you going to do?'

'I'm off to Florida,' he said, the slight trace of a smile on his lips.

Not bad. He gets to bugger off to the States and leave us to do the groundwork? I didn't mind though. The case sounded huge. Infiltrating the Colombian cartels? Exposing a corrupt bank? Global operation? This was massive.

The first thing I did was 'house' our target. Colin and I got an address for Baakza and checked it out. He lived in Brent Cross, north London. We cross referenced the electoral roll and he was still registered there. I pulled his passport application. He was a British citizen of Pakistani origin. We now had a photo of him, but it was nearly ten years out of date. At least it gave us a vague idea of who we were looking for.

The following morning, we were in his street at 6am to start establishing his pattern. I was living in Tottenham, so it was a 30-minute drive around the North Circular. It was a typically quiet, suburban street. We checked out the house – a well-presented, semi-detached, family home, I imagined an estate agent blurb might say.

It was a little too quiet for my liking, so we parked as far away as we could, while still having eyeball on the front door. It was impossible to look completely inconspicuous, but at least any nosy neighbours wouldn't know why we were there.

At around 7.30am a man opened the front door. He was short, only five-foot-six-inches tall, slight, with jet-black hair and a small moustache. He was dressed like a typical banker, suited, with a shirt and tie, carrying a briefcase, and looked pretty much the same as his passport photo. He headed off in the direction of Brent Cross underground station. We didn't follow him. Don't show out, Bruce had said. Most likely, he would get the Northern Line to Bank and walk the short distance to Leadenhall Street. We'd watch the office later and look for him leaving. There was no rush. We had time to build up a picture of this guy.

Back in the office I began researching BCCI. It had only been going since 1972, but in sixteen years had grown to become the seventh-largest private bank in the world, with over 400 branches in 78 countries. It was founded by a Pakistani financier called Agha Hasan Abedi, with 75 per cent capital from Sheikh Zayed bin Sultan Al Nahyan, the ruler of Abu Dhabi in the United Arab Emirates, and the remaining 25 per cent from the Bank of America. Although the bank was formally registered in Luxembourg, it had two head offices – the one in Leadenhall Street, London and another in Karachi, Pakistan.

Baakza's office was, in some ways, an easier watch. We had to stand outside but, with thousands of people around and lots of street cover, we blended into the background. Shortly after 6.30pm, our target appeared. While other bank workers emerged in twos or threes and headed to bars, restaurants or shops, he emerged alone and, head down, made off in the direction of the Bank of England. We watched, just to make sure he was heading for the underground station, and then let him go.

We continued this pattern for three weeks, making sure he stuck to the same routine, which he did. He seemed a creature of habit, who rose for work and returned home at pretty much the same time every night. He was married, but we only caught a brief glimpse of his wife once.

During the three weeks, Bruce would call from Florida asking us to do various other checks, so we investigated Baakza's tax returns and bank accounts for any unusual activity or sudden appearances of additional income, which might further suggest corrupt practices. We checked what he was paying for his house, whether he was up to date with his rates and taxes. There was nothing out of the ordinary.

Bruce returned from Florida and put in an application to Alpha, the first of its kind I had seen. It asked for a facility on all telephone numbers for Baakza. As Bruce sat at his word processor and typed it out, it was the first time I saw the name of this international investigation: Operation C-Chase.

The application stated that US Customs had penetrated the Colombian drug cartels and established that one of the banks illicit money was going into was the BCCI. Baakza was named as the banker who was helping the cartels. Bruce had already logged the banker as our target on CEDRIC – giving both our names as contacts – so the operational teams and New Scotland Yard saw that he was a person of interest. Our surveillance had shown nothing out of the ordinary, but the hope was that telephone intercepts could established how big a player he truly was. It could have been amazing intelligence. We would never find out. Alpha refused the application. Perhaps, at that stage, a major money laundering case was seen as far too complex and a much lower priority than an operational drugs investigation.

Bruce flew back out to Florida and for the next few weeks it was more of the same – monitoring Baakza from a safe distance, working on tasks Bruce set us from afar, completing any checks that needed to be made. Bruce gave nothing away about what was happening in the States, only that the investigation was already well advanced.

When he next returned to the UK, there had been some developments. The undercover agents had made real progress, successfully laundering millions of dollars on behalf of the most notorious of drug smuggling gangs and gathering evidence showing institutionalised corruption at BCCI. They were entering the final stages of the investigation and arrests were imminent.

But that wasn't all. The coup de grâce was going to be an ultra-ambitious takedown of the bent bankers, money launderers and drug dealers. The agent's plan was to stage a fake wedding. He claimed he and his undercover-agent colleague were getting married. He had told his contacts they were engaged, after all. The nuptials would be in Tampa, Florida, where the investigation started and where BCCI had an office, and he would invite the bank's officers, representatives from the Colombian cartels and drug dealers from around the world that he had befriended and secured evidence on during his mammoth operation that had now been going on for nearly two years.

It was staggering in its scale. The plan, if it came off, would be one of the biggest attacks on organised crime in decades, and it would send shockwaves through the cartels, the banking system and every investor in BCCI.

There was an additional significant development for our team too. The investigation had broadened from focusing only on BCCI to also include a commodities futures firm called Capcom, which had offices in London and Chicago. I was aware that it traded a lot in metals and was particularly active on the Chicago stock exchange. It had only been operating since 1984 and there was a strong link to the BCCI. It was created by the former head of BCCI's treasury department, Ziauddin Ali Akbar, known to us as Tango Two, who capitalised it with funds from BCCI and its customers.

Bruce said the undercover officer was coming to London on 18 September, specifically to visit Capcom's office in the city. He told us to arrange an observation point near Capcom, in Snow Hill, so we could photograph the officer going in and monitor the meeting.

Colin and I checked out the Capcom address. It was in a small, brown-brick building, not far from the Old Bailey. There was an empty office across the street from it. When we fed this back, our technical team – the same one that planted bugs in hotel rooms – was tasked with the job of getting us inside that vacant office space.

John le Carré called them the lamplighters – the section of his fictionalised MI6 responsible for surveillance and wiretapping – and every service has them. In this instance, the technical team effectively broke into the office, secured it and made it ours for the three days we would need it to properly surveil the meeting. Once they'd done their work, we got in there a couple of days before the meeting was due to take place and set up a camera, training it on the Capcom door.

On the day the undercover officer was due to arrive, Walt got a call from immigration at Heathrow.

'Fucking hell,' he said, once he came off the phone. 'The Yank undercover has been arrested on a dodgy passport.'

Now we had a name. Robert Mazur. He had flown in on Concorde along with the female officer who was posing as his fiancée. When he handed over his passport, the immigration inspector spotted immediately it was fake. A previous UK stamp had the wrong emblem on it. Every two years UK immigration changed the emblem on the stamps and the date in Mazur's passport didn't match the design used at that time. He was in big trouble.

We later heard that the FBI had been responsible for creating his fake document. They had assured him he wouldn't be compromised.

Mazur was ordered to strip and very nearly subjected to a full internal search. It was only when his specially modified briefcase, in which an $8,000 Nagra recorder had been hidden, was about to be ripped apart by an inspector that he came clean about his identity and offered to show them the covert device before they destroyed his bag. He told them he was an undercover US Customs agent working on a case in London with their Customs colleagues.

It's fair to say the response he got was one of incredulity. To the inspectors, who had heard it all, this was just another conman. He had to give the name of his contact at the US embassy, John Luksic, who was liaising with Bruce. While all this was going on, Kathy Ertz, the agent pretending to be his 'fiancée' had been detained awaiting his release.

As it turned out, Mazur had been unlucky. A recent incident involving Korean espionage had led to a heightened state of alert at the UK's airports. John Luksic went to meet the staff to vouch for his story, and it was confirmed by Walt who was ex-Heathrow, and the undercover officers were allowed to enter the country.

Bruce met with Mazur and Luksic the following morning to go over the plan for the Capcom meeting. Luksic told the undercover officer our observation point was already in place and that we would be on his tail for the duration of his stay. Bruce assured them any surveillance would be inobtrusive and in no way compromise his operation. After what had happened at Heathrow, we didn't want to give him any more scares.

The following day, Colin and I got to Snow Hill early to make sure everything was in place for the meeting. Colin set up a tripod. We didn't know what was going to be evidential. We had no intelligence about who might turn up, who to look out for. For all we knew Pablo Escobar himself might show up. We were working on the basis of photographing everyone.

At the back of our mind was the slight risk that someone from the building we had commandeered might appear, demanding to know who we were and what we were doing, but we were confident about dealing with such an eventuality with the minimum of fuss.

We watched as the business of the day at Capcom unfolded, photographing everyone who came and went, until we got word that the meeting had concluded and we could pack up. We then returned to the office and Colin handed over the rolls of film to be developed. This was all done in-house by the technical team, as was any computer forensics.

Now that Bruce had met Mazur, he had a greater understanding of what was happening. A date had been set for the fake wedding – Sunday 9 October.

The beauty of the scam was its simplicity. Most of the targets either resided in, or had had the means to flee to, countries without extradition treaties with the United States, like Pakistan or Colombia. Trying to arrest the suspects on their own soil was an impossible mission. By inviting the targets to Tampa, it meant they could arrest them in one swoop, on their home patch.

The targets had been told the wedding was taking place at the exclusive Innisbrook Golf Resort in Tampa, just the sort of location a well-heeled money launderer would tie the knot. The 'guests' would be arriving on the Friday and Saturday, October 7 and 8, and would enjoy an early evening poolside cocktail party, before congregating on the Sunday morning for the wedding ceremony that was due to start at 10am. The arrests were due to take place during the ceremony.

US Customs had it all worked out. As the Monday was going to be a federal holiday, they were planning the press conference, to announce the success of the operation, on Tuesday, to be chaired by their commissioner William von Raab. They had requested someone from our end be there, along with French Customs, who were working on a BCCI angle in Paris. Our ACIO, Geoff Heslop, decided he, naturally, should be there. The Americans were going to have the wedding dress and the gifts from the criminal guests on display. It promised to be quite a show.

While they were giving their wedding guests the shock of their lives, raids would take place on BCCI offices in Tampa, Panama and Paris. We would raid the office in Leadenhall Street. There was also talk of another team hitting the Capcom office we had watched.

Their plan for us sounded simple. We needed to be primed to arrest Baakza at 7.30am UK time. This was a few hours earlier than the agents would be reading the wedding guests their rights in Tampa, but if we left it until 3pm to coordinate the knocks there was a chance Baakza could already be out for the day. Taking out Baakza early was less likely to compromise the operation. If the US jumped the gun, however, and Baakza was spooked, we might have a problem. We would therefore be outside his door before 6am. If he left his house before 7.30am we would arrest him anyway. Until then, we simply had to make sure everything went as normal with Baakza and that we knew he would be at home come the morning of the knock.

It sounded quite straightforward – which perhaps should have been an indication that things would inevitably go wrong.

Sure enough, in the days leading up to the wedding there were some added complications. Nazir Chinoy, the head of BCCI operations in French-speaking countries and a key corrupt bank executive that Mazur had met in Paris, called him to say he couldn't attend the wedding. He was required to be at a board meeting in London. He sent along two associates instead, with his gift to the happy couple – a $40,000 one-of-a-kind Persian rug.

That change of plan meant UK Customs would have to arrest Chinoy – now our Tango Three – in the capital before he had a chance to flee the country. Tango Two – Ziauddin Ali Akbar – would also be arrested at the same time

On the day before the arrests were due to take place, we held a pre-knock briefing. I was to go with Bruce to Baakza's house at 5am to get ready to arrest him and take him to Bishopsgate Police Station, where he'd be interviewed under caution. Steve Berry would sit outside his house all night, in the event of any last-minute change of plan. He was going to take the one office mobile phone we had – a huge thing with a big shoulder bag.

Once we'd arrested Tango One, a team would go to the BCCI offices with the search warrant and begin scouring Baakza's office for any incriminating documents.

Two other teams were formed to arrest Chinoy and Akbar and search any cars, Akbar's home and Capcom.

I went to bed that night buzzing for the day ahead. This was why I had joined the Investigation Division. I could tell this case was going to big – something that might fill newspaper pages and books for years to come. It was always at the back of my mind though that there couldn't be any cock-ups from our end. The last thing I wanted was to be the guy who lost the main man in the UK.

What we didn't know, was that over in Florida, a power struggle was playing out that would alter the plan dramatically.

||

Shortly before Mazur had left for Europe to tie up the loose ends in his investigation, he became aware that senior US Customs officials were speaking to NBC News, one of the big TV networks there. Bill Rosenblatt, the assistant commissioner of enforcement for Customs, and Bonni Tischler, ambitious head of the Tampa field office where Mazur was based, had met with a producer and investigative reporter from NBC and given them an outline of the undercover operation.

Mazur was, understandably, seething. He and Kathy Ertz were putting their lives on the line and their bosses were leaking to the media. Any of the criminals whose confidence and trust they had earned would have killed them in an instant had they known they were federal agents.

The belief among the US Customs rank and file was that Commissioner von Raab, Rosenblatt and Tischler wanted as much publicity as possible, one assumed to further their careers. Obviously it wasn't enough for them to have the glitzy press conference to the world's media two days after the arrests. They wanted something more explosive, it seemed.

And, so, the plan changed. Von Raab and Rosenblatt offered NBC News exclusive coverage of the wedding ceremony. NBC cameramen were to pose as videographers capturing the happy nuptials.

Senior Customs officers pushed back on this change. There had already been a fear among the investigators that the original plan – arresting the criminals in a massive public takedown involving 50 agents or more – might be unnecessarily stressful on the targets' wives and children, also guests at the wedding, who were after all innocent parties.

An alternative plan was drawn up. As the poolside cocktail party on the Saturday night ended, limousines would take the suspects to a club 25 miles away from the resort, under the pretence that they were heading to a surprise bachelor party for Mazur. This provided the perfect ruse to lure the targets away from their families, and bought time for the Customs agents to make the arrests away from the resort and then calmly approach the families afterwards to notify them of what happened.

Although much consideration had been given to how the news would be broken to the shocked families, none was given to Customs on this side of the Atlantic, nor to Heslop, who didn't cover himself in glory by being out of the loop about the arrests. We all went to bed with no knowledge of the fake bachelor party, or any change to the plans.

We were as much in the dark as the drug traffickers, money launderers and bent bankers from all over the world who began descending on the Innisbrook club on Friday. They arrived to find the resort's plush Harstan Lawn wedding venue had been lavishly prepared for the following day's ceremony, with no expense spared. Inside an extravagant, white marquee, a scarlet carpet, with 125 chairs set out on either side, ran to a specially prepared altar, which was to be decorated with $20,000 worth of Colombian red roses – a gift from one of the guests, Juan Tobon. He was the son of a former mayor of Medellín, the city where Pablo Escobar built his feared cartel.

Mazur and Ertz did have a last-minute hitch to contend with. Rudolf Armbrecht, a Colombian businessman and major organiser for the Medellín cartel, failed to arrive in Tampa on Saturday. When Ertz called him, she found he was in a hotel in Miami, planning to arrive at the wedding for the ceremony the following morning, and therefore missing the Friday night plans. While she kept him on the phone talking, agents stormed his room and arrested him. He was the first to go down.

When it was time to take the 'wedding guests' to the bachelor party, Customs agents guided the targets into their limos. They were none the wiser when they pulled up at the car park of the Exchange Bank building in downtown Tampa, where MacBeth's club occupied the top floor. Instead of taking the elevator to the 26th floor and the club, an undercover DEA agent took them instead to the third floor, where armed agents were waiting.

Even when they were under arrest, some of the targets were so much in the dark about the ruse that they asked that a message be passed to Mazur, expressing their regret that they wouldn't be able to attend his wedding, and asking after his own fate. Another thought the presence of the police was some sort of stripper act.

On his way to the club, one suspect asked an undercover agent in his limo if there was a chance he could get laid at the bachelor party. 'I can assure you, you're going to get fucked tonight like you've never been fucked before,' the agent replied.

The feeling of being done over by US Customs was one I could relate to – especially at that moment I was woken at 3am by Control.

We will never know what prompted Baakza to decide to flee in the middle of the night. Who called him? Who managed to get word out from Tampa? If Alpha hadn't rejected our request to monitor his calls, we would have known. For all the benefits their team gave Customs, in the end it was good, old-fashioned law enforcement that rescued the situation. Having someone as brilliant as Steve outside the house saved us.

There was so much going on as we started searching the BCCI office – after dealing with the issue of the incorrect address – alongside the other team from Customs, suspiciously headed up by the very senior Ian Stewart. I had no time to properly raise my queries with my senior colleagues. Colleagues had successfully detained Akbar and also raided the Capcom offices. Chinoy was swept up later.

We quickly analysed some of the seized material and then, together with Henry Black and Jack – who would question Akbar – Bruce and I headed to Bishopsgate Police Station to finally meet the man I had been watching for months.

CHAPTER 8

|||||||||||||||||||||||||||||||||||||||||||

The suspect

The clock was ticking. Under the Police and Criminal Evidence Act 1984, it started running as soon as we arrested Asif Baakza. We had 24 hours before we had to charge or release him but, as he'd been arrested at 3am, a chunk of that time had already elapsed, and we also had to wait for his lawyer to show up at Bishopsgate Police Station.

Plus, at the back of my mind I still had the sight of Walt jumping up and down – both about the Americans and our warrant cock-up. At least we were off to a good start with our suspect. Doing a runner in the middle of the night was good evidence, bearing in mind events in Tampa.

On our BITs course we were taught that two main things were needed for a conviction – *mens rea*, a guilty mind, and *actus reus*, a guilty act. Those were the two main ingredients for a criminal offence. What would a jury think of a banker coming out of his house at 3am, in the context of a raid going on in Florida that night? If Baakza was able to produce a flight ticket to Pakistan, booked weeks earlier, he might be able to show his actions were purely coincidental. We would soon find out.

Before we commenced the interview, Bruce and I went through the available seized evidence, which included a physical record of a transaction for the right amount, near his desk.

That was a start. Bruce briefed me that, during his meeting with Mazur, Baakza had been told that it was cocaine proceeds he was being asked to move in this transaction, and he had agreed to this.

We went through his paper diary to check whether there was a record of the meeting or whether he had Mazur's number in his contacts. Bruce then told me that the pseudonym Mazur had used was Bob Musella.

The interview was only going to be about the one transaction. It didn't seem like much, but it would be enough to send him to prison, if a jury found him guilty.

What we had to prove was that Baakza knew or suspected he was moving drugs money. We might have a physical record of the transaction, but that level of knowledge could not be found on the paper record.

Five hours after we had commenced the search of Baakza's office, Bruce and I got word that his lawyer, a brief from the big City corporate firm Stephenson Harwood, most likely arranged by his employer, had arrived. We could begin the interview.

Bruce, the senior investigator, only had one piece of advice for me: 'Keep your mouth shut.' Other than that, I went in equipped with some holding questions, if needed, to allow Bruce time to gather his thoughts and to get myself on tape, so it looked like I'd played a part if I was ever needed to give evidence in the States later.

The first thing that struck me, as we sat down to start the interview, was how cool Baakza was. If his insides were in turmoil, he didn't show it. There was not an ounce of emotion, not a bead of sweat. Perhaps he had no idea about the seriousness of the situation, perhaps he genuinely believed he hadn't done anything wrong, but his calmness in the face of extreme pressure was fascinating to observe.

I had to keep reminding myself that he had left his house in the middle of the night, to go where, we had no idea, but something had prompted him to act hastily. Without knowing that about him, I might have been led to believe that he hadn't a clue why he was there.

As Bruce worked through the questions, starting first with a request for some basic, personal information about him, Baakza he seemed perfectly pleasant. When we came onto Bob Musella, I thought we might see some reaction, perhaps a little flicker of panic. There was nothing. He remained as cool as a cucumber.

He confirmed that he had met with an individual who had asked him to move $10,000.

Bruce said: 'I have to tell you that guy was an undercover American Customs officer.'

Again, he didn't flinch. He didn't fall apart. He simply didn't respond.

Bruce then went on to put it to Baakza that it was made clear to him the money in question was the proceeds of cocaine smuggling. 'You knew that,' he said. 'What's your response?'

Again, he didn't give anything away.

I kept thinking of what we were taught in our BITs course. During an interview with our suspects, where confessions don't exist, we were looking for two main things – provable lies, or forensics. A provable lie is when someone tells you a falsehood that you can later disprove. If he had said to us that he had never met Mazur in his life we would have been able to disprove that. But he didn't. He knew the transaction was documented and, by now, he would have suspected that the meeting was documented.

I imagined that at the back of his mind he was thinking about the intelligence he received. Was it to leave the country, or start shredding? That he was unable to do either was probably influencing his tactics now.

Forensics, such as fingerprints on a box of drugs, weren't applicable here. The paper trail showed the transaction took place and the meeting with Mazur wasn't in doubt. The case would likely come down to the strength of Mazur's tape recording.

The interview lasted several hours and in that time we stopped for breaks and refreshments. Baakza's lawyer was content to let the questions flow, and didn't step in to advise his client. It was all very calm and cordial.

It did cross my mind that if the bank did arrange for the lawyer, their interests and Baakza's might not coincide. It occurred to me that perhaps the person before us was not that senior and it was just his bad fortune that he was the one asked to look after Mazur. Maybe he was just doing what he was told – and it could have been any BCCI banker sitting before us. If that was the case, he might have considered speaking up, explaining his innocence in the whole matter and passing the blame to a more senior colleague, but he said nothing material. Did he hope his omertà would be looked on favourably?

Whatever his reasons, he stuck to his strategy and, by the end of it, we were no further forward, really, apart from giving him the chance to explain himself.

Aside from the tape and record of the transaction, the best evidence we had was that he had left his house at 3am. He had no real explanation for that and didn't produce any previously booked air tickets.

I got the impression Bruce was expecting more, even if it was just some sort of reaction, but Baakza didn't flinch once.

As the interview closed, we charged him, and the same was done to Akbar. That was the reason Bruce chose to interview him in a police station. We could have conducted it at Custom House, but only had the power to charge him in a police station.

Even when Bruce put it to Baakza that he was charging him with laundering the proceeds of drugs, he showed no emotion. He was detained in custody, and he would appear before a magistrate in the morning.

When our business at Bishopsgate concluded, Bruce and I returned to the office, where all the documents relating to Baakza and others that had been seized from BCCI were on our desks. That was going to be our task for the weeks and months ahead – sifting through this and the mountain of paperwork we expected to receive from US Customs.

I returned home that night exhausted from a long and tiring day but energised for the next stage in the investigation.

There was a footnote to the day's proceedings. While we had been waiting for Baakza's lawyer to appear at Bishopsgate, I couldn't help but notice an attractive, bleached-blonde police-woman who said, 'hi', as we passed. During the day, whenever we stopped for a break, I saw her coming and going. I discovered her name was Rebecca and she was a detective constable. Like many of her colleagues, she was intrigued by our presence at the station. To them, having Customs officers conduct an interview on a money laundering case on their doorstep was highly unusual.

The following day I rang the station to find out she was next on duty during that night's evening shift. I called Bishopsgate after 9pm and spoke to her. At first she thought it was a wind up, but after establishing I really was the six-foot Customs guy she'd greeted yesterday, I asked her on a date and, to my delight, she said yes. I remember asking the stylish Carol on the Whisky team what an ideal gift might be to take a southerner for a first date. I was considering a single rose but wondered if it was a bit clichéd. She recommended a single boxed orchid, so I bought one from the posh florists in Leadenhall Market. It seemed to do the trick because we dated for a few months after that.

It might have been the day of the wedding that never was, but that didn't have to mean romance couldn't blossom elsewhere.

CHAPTER 9

Stitch-up

'Is that it?' That was my first reaction when I finally listened to the tape of Robert Mazur's meeting with Asif Baakza. 'This is bullshit.'

The banker was barely audible. The so-called damning evidence was questionable, to say the least. If this was what the case was hanging on, we might have trouble convincing a jury of his guilt.

Only when we began to sift through the evidence on C-Chase, minus the mysterious material seized by the other team at BCCI, did I fully start to appreciate the scale of the operation.

Mazur had recorded so many hours of tape it would take a dozen transcribers more than a year to transcribe and proof all the conversations. The one we were interested in was a miniscule part of that and took place at the Portman Hotel, a typically expensive establishment, on Portman Square in central London on 26 May.

This was the first time Mazur met with Baakza. Mazur and his 'fiancee' Kathy Ertz had travelled from Paris to the meeting in the UK by ferry, where the immigration officials perhaps weren't as eagle-eyed as they were at Heathrow.

The agents checked into the hotel on 26 May and Mazur arranged to meet Baakza for lunch the following day, but the banker cancelled. Instead, they met later that same day, at 6pm in Mazur's hotel room. The agent wanted Baakza to meet Ertz too, because she would have power of attorney, should anything happen to Mazur.

'What we need to accomplish has to do with the placement and transfer of funds in a very, very confidential and secure fashion,' Mazur said.

The banker explained that BCCI London offered a manager's ledger account to customers seeking total privacy. He compared it to a numbered account in Switzerland. Only he and one other individual in the bank would have access to Mazur's records.

Baakza added: 'I don't want to know anything that I don't need to know. It's as simple as that.'

Mazur said that his clients were mostly respectable Colombians. By way of comparison, he used a ploy he had tried out on Chinoy in Paris.

'Really, I think that if they were in the same room with Lee Iacocca, they probably would be taken as being corporate executives with Chrysler,' Mazur said. 'It's just that they aren't in that business and, you know, these people are very, very feared people. That's why I made sure I researched everything to the nth degree before I actually moved here.'

Baakza said: 'Uh-huh.'

'When you're dealing with the most powerful men in Colombia, who are involved in drug dealing, you need to make sure you know what you're doing,' Mazur went on.

'Hmm,' Baakza replied.

'Iacocca sells cars and they sell coke. And that's the only difference. But they're executives about the whole thing.'

Baakza didn't reply.

That was the extent of the meeting – and it was the only one Mazur held with Baakza.

I listened to the tape of the meeting, thinking, *this is essentially a stitch-up*. Surely a good defence lawyer would get him off. He was barely audible. There was only a faint agreement with what Mazur, who was clearly trying to transfer suspicion, had said.

I thought back again to our training. We were always told to never prompt someone into committing a crime. They must guide you. In my mind this was a case of an agent provocateur leading the target.

I would have felt less queasy and more confident of a conviction had Baakza proactively offered to help Mazur move his cash to London, not just responded to the undercover officer's suggestions. But, for the agent to make a reference to Lee Iacocca, the CEO of Chrysler, and draw a comparison from him to his clients ... was it clear what Baakza was agreeing to?

The fact that Mazur referred to 'coke', rather than 'cocaine', made me feel uneasy. Pepsi sold cola in Colombia, which was commonly known as 'coke'. A good criminal defence lawyer would surely slaughter all this. Mazur was the one leading the conversation, not Baakza. It felt like the banker was being stitched up – and we were not allowed to do that. I just couldn't escape the feeling that the banker was a lamb to the slaughter. How big a player was he? Or how much was he just doing his boss's bidding? Something just wasn't right. It would be for a jury to decide however, because there was no going back now.

We didn't yet have sight of the full US Customs case, but I had seen enough to think this couldn't just be about $10,000 worth of US treasury money being passed off as drug money. That was peanuts. The London BCCI connection had to be part of something far bigger.

We knew Mazur had been laundering millions for the Colombians through BCCI in Florida, Panama and Paris but what was so significant about this little additional transaction in London? It didn't add up.

I thought back to the presence of Ian Stewart and his team in the BCCI building. Why were they there?

The arrests had generated a lot of media coverage, predictably. How often did Customs officers – or anyone – raid a bank's HQ? The initial coverage was all about the scale of the US investigation but there was already some speculation about what it could mean for the bank's future.

I voiced my concerns to Steve Berry. Of the senior officers, he was one I'd built up a strong connection with. With his usual sardonic wit, he was a popular guy and didn't take matters as seriously as some of the others. He was puffing on a fag when I bent his ear about Baakza.

'What was all that at the bank with Stewart's team?' I asked him. 'And where's all the material they nabbed?'

'You know it's all political, don't you?'

'What do you mean?'

'It's all come down from Thatcher,' he said.

'How so?'

'Your man ... he's not just someone who moved some dodgy cash. He's Noriega's London banker. Or one of them, at least.'

'Noriega?'

I knew who he meant, of course. General Manuel Noriega, the de facto ruler of Panama, had been an ally of the United

States and enjoyed a long association with the CIA but, from following the news, I knew the Americans had suspected him of feeding intelligence to their sworn enemy, Fidel Castro in Cuba, and had accused him of being in league with the Colombian drug cartels.

'Now it makes sense,' I said.

'Stewart was after evidence on Noriega. One of the others that was arrested here … he was Noriega's main man. But your guy, Baakza, was the next in line. He handled the transactions, they believe.'

'You said it all came from Margaret Thatcher.'

Steve nodded.

'It's the presidential elections next month. George Bush, Reagan's vice president, is standing. So, he called Thatcher and asked her to do him a little favour.'

Vice president George H.W. Bush had a vested interest in wanting to uncover as much evidence on Manuel Noriega as possible. The war on drugs had been a feature of Ronald Reagan's presidency ever since First Lady Nancy's 'Just Say No' advertising campaign in the early eighties. Although the campaign did much to warn ordinary Americans about the dangers of recreational drugs, the reality was that more narcotics were flooding into the US than ever before.

One of the main proponents driving the drug trade was Manuel Noriega, who had been effectively leasing Panama to the cocaine smugglers, particularly Pablo Escobar's Medellín cartel, as a staging post for their US-bound product.

Noriega was also permitting banks in Panama to wash billions of dollars of cocaine cash. It was therefore no coincidence that BCCI had twelve branches in this tiny Central American country, which only had a population of 3 million people.

What had probably gone unspoken during George Bush's phone call to the British prime minister was how Noriega had been on the CIA's agent payroll for years, as a conduit for American funds and weapons to Contra rebels in Nicaragua, including when Bush was the agency's boss.

Also unsaid would have been how extraditing and prosecuting Noriega would be a massive boost for Bush's election campaign and putting him behind bars in an American prison would also silence a major source of embarrassment for the candidate.

But he had a big, big problem. Noriega's vast illicit cash – much of it from Pablo Escobar – and his secrets, were in the City of London, at the BCCI's Leadenhall Street HQ. This is where much of the evidence needed to convict Noriega before a US jury was hidden.

It was Bush, Steve said, who told Thatcher about the US Customs service's international, covert investigation.

The date that had been set for the fake wedding was no coincidence. The US government had put pressure on Customs bosses to have it wrapped up no later than early October. The raids on BCCI, the arrest of bankers and the discovery of Noriega's illicit drug cash would be a timely coup just before the presidential elections. As it turned out, the arrests in Tampa took place exactly one month ahead of the US poll on 8 November.

'It's all about Noriega,' Steve said.

That explained everything.

As more evidence came to light in the British and French ends of the investigation, it became apparent how Baakza came to be an integral part of the operation.

Back in November 1987, Mazur's covert money laundering business was already up and running and was paying the

Colombian cartel in cheques drawn on BCCI Panama. His cheques were then being handed, via his money men contacts, to the cartel drug smugglers.

Then fortune smiled on Mazur. Syed Aftab Hussain, of BCCI Panama, contacted Mazur to raise an issue with two cheques that had been brought to them by one of Mazur's clients. On one cheque the payee had been left blank, while, on the other, the written amount to be cashed didn't match with the numerical amount. Hussain wanted to know which amount to pay to Mazur's customer.

It had been a mistake on Mazur's part. The blank cheques had been smuggled into Colombia. While he worked out how to answer, Hussein offered a solution. He offered to authorise any cheques passed through the bank.

The presence of the dodgy cheques indicated to the bank that Mazur was a money launderer. However, instead of closing his accounts and refusing to do business with him, they were offering to help him do business more efficiently. Hussain told Mazur, in words that would come back to haunt BCCI: 'We are a full-service bank.'

When Mazur met Hussain later, in Miami, the BCCI official, remarkably, advised him how to launder money better. Hussain also gave the Customs agent the name of a high-ranking regional officer of the bank and the former manager of BCCI Panama, who still handled Panamanian accounts like Mazur's. Amjad Awan was the man Mazur needed to meet, and in January 1988, again in Miami, Hussain set it up. Awan, it would transpire, was one of the top money laundering targets in the world.

And one customer, in particular, took advantage of his expertise.

General Noriega began his association with Awan and BCCI in January 1982, with a deposit of $100,000. He followed that up with large deposits every two or three months, into several secret numbered accounts. Sometime, around the middle of 1983, the general asked that his accounts be moved from Panama to the BCCI in London, as Awan advised him that he thought they would be able to maintain greater confidentiality there.

Noriega continued to deposit increasingly large sums of money into several accounts.

Awan was transferred by BCCI to Washington and Miami, but continued to oversee the general's finances. Then, in September 1984, the bank agreed to lend Noriega $400,000 to buy a flat in Paris. The loan was paid off in less than six months, mostly by interest accruing from his four main accounts at BCCI.

Over those years, from 1982 to 1988, Noriega and his family deposited at least $23 million into secret BCCI accounts. Some individual cash deposits were as large as $3.4 million. The enterprise lasted until February 1988, when he was indicted by two grand juries in Florida on charges of cocaine trafficking, racketeering and money laundering.

As a colonel in the Panamanian armed forces in the early 1980s, Noriega's salary was only about $30,000 a year. Even after he became commander-in-chief of the Panama Defence Forces in August 1983, he would have been paid an official annual salary of about $50,000. The source of his wealth, besides proceeds of cocaine trafficking, was at least $10 million paid to him by US intelligence services.

When the indictment was served on him, Noriega asked that his British accounts be closed and the funds, which at the time amounted to $19.3 million, be transferred back to Panama. Awan convinced the general he would be better moving the money to Luxembourg, where there was more banking secrecy, even than in Britain.

Within months, Noriega and his wife, Felicidad Sieiro de Noriega, moved all their BCCI wealth, a total of $23 million, to banks in Switzerland and Germany. Not long after, the money was moved again, to Capcom in London, before it was transferred to yet another bank.

This was around the same time that Mazur's bogus enterprise was sending $2 million a month to Awan for Panama accounts controlled by his cartel clients in Medellín. As the bond between them grew, Awan offered to help facilitate Mazur's requests in other BCCI offices, including Paris and London. While in the French capital, meeting with BCCI officials there, Mazur took a call from Awan who told him he was visiting 'a dear friend in London'. The friend was Awan's contact at BCCI London, Asif Baakza.

'My friend is ready to greet you,' Awan said.

That was the moment Baakza's fate was sealed.

CHAPTER 10

IIIIIIIIIIIIIIIIIIIIIIIIIIIIIIIIIIIIIIII

'90 per cent office, 10 per cent fun'

In the weeks following the BCCI arrests, I was working flat out. We had a committal hearing looming at the magistrate court and that was my sole focus.

There was a lot to do. We had to prepare evidence to show there was a *prima facie* – on the face of it – case against Baakza and Akbar, and we had to persuade the court the case was strong enough to go to trial. If we succeeded, the magistrate would send the case to the crown court.

To prepare for this, we worked closely with our own Solicitors' Office, which was something unique in British law. In theory, it was them who decided whether to charge someone or not.

Unlike the police, which refers to the Crown Prosecution Service, as a separate body, Customs had their own lawyers. The legal case officer for C-Chase was the bubbly Diana Bowers, a barrister by training. Bruce and I personally took the evidence across to her as often as we could and she formally served it on the defence and prepared papers for the court.

By the nature of the relationship between investigators and solicitors, the legal service was not wholly independent. The Solicitors' Office attracted earnest and dedicated lawyers, but why would you work for Customs for only £40,000 a year when you could be earning £400,000 in a law firm? Some lawyers had barrister partners also specialising in VAT fraud, and they would instruct them to work on a case. Barrister's fees for a complex VAT fraud could top £1 million easily.

One of the most powerful in the office was the Honourable Annabelle Bolt, which demonstrated it could attract posh, privileged figures, but the fact that Customs cases were driven by the investigators, not the lawyers, was still a bone of contention. A key example of this was the fact that lawyers were never told if Alpha was involved in an operation, and investigators mostly decided if suspects were to be charged, like on C-Chase. Similarly, the police have the power to charge lower-level crimes, but bigger cases are referred to the Crown Prosecution Service.

The Solicitors' Office was the most expensive post office in the country. Material came in from investigators and they sent it out to court without much attention or analysis. It was based at Customs' official headquarters in Sea Containers House, on the South Bank, where the Board of HM Customs had its offices.

Once she was satisfied we had enough evidence for committal, Diana instructed a senior barrister to prosecute, which in this instance was Nigel Peters QC. Her husband was named as junior counsel to assist.

To prepare the case for court we had to go through hundreds of documents and computer records. Baakza's and Akbar's involvements were minimal and the transactions simple ones, but the paperwork was still considerable. We had the tapes transcribed and arranged a witness statement from Mazur explaining the whole process that led to the meetings in London and confirming that the transcription was an accurate record of what took place. We also had to arrange witness statements from everyone on the team who had taken part in surveillance and/or removed documents from the bank, Capcom and the defendants' home addresses. It was laborious, time-consuming work.

However, once we saw the chain of evidence, and followed the money coming into BCCI, then going into an account Mazur had asked to be set up, that was pretty much all we needed, along with the covert tape recordings and post-arrest interviews.

At this stage, nothing in the court documents related to Noriega.

Since his personal intervention, George H.W. Bush had won the presidential election, as expected, but with an electoral college and popular vote majority that few could have predicted. His aggressive campaign, which focused heavily on being tough on urban crime, including drugs, and continuing Reagan's international agenda, went down well with voters. Now he was president, he could ramp up his offensive against his one-time ally.

The raids on BCCI and Capcom had resulted in lorry-loads of documents being seized. A thorough examination of the paperwork might reveal evidence of BCCI's involvement with the Panamanian leader, but it also might expose the bank's connections to both the political and intelligence communities on either side of the Atlantic. *Private Eye* reported that BCCI was not just the go-to bank for drug smugglers; it was used by MI6 and CIA to launder money to the Afghan mujahideen to fight the Soviets for years.

However, until we were instructed otherwise, our focus was on Baakza. The committal hearings for his case, and that of Ziauddin Akbar, were held several months later and, for them both, Mazur was required to testify.

His welcome to the UK for the court dates was slightly different to his last experience at Heathrow. This time, armed officers from the City of London Police anti-terrorism squad collected him from the airport and took him at high speed, with blue lights flashing, to the force's headquarters, which would be his home for the duration of the hearings. A secret tunnel enabled him to arrive at the court without being detected.

There was good reason to be cautious. Since the arrests at the wedding, a suspect package had been found in the Tampa Customs office. Given that Escobar had been bombing anyone who stood in his way in Colombia, Mazur feared the cartel boss would be able to export terrorism just as easily as he exported cocaine. Mazur had also been required to change his identity after a breathtaking security breach from a colleague in the Internal Revenue Service (IRS), who gave his real name to a defence lawyer in Tampa. Mazur, who had spent the last two years pretending to be someone else as part of his job, now had to do it for his own safety, particularly as some of the people he helped arrest claimed there was a $500,000 contract on his head and a hit squad was on its way from Colombia to carry it out.

While he moved his family to a safe location and his children's school records were securely sealed, another Robert Mazur, who lived in the same town and was listed in the phone book, was alerted to the potential problems the unfortunate coincidence might bring his way.

The hearing at the magistrates' court was the first time the Customs agent had seen Baakza since their meeting to discuss the transaction. Mazur has since described how the banker's eyes looked 'sunken in his skull and lined in black hatred', as well they might have been, given that it was a conversation that changed his life.

Mazur's testimony, together with the case our lawyers prepared, and the investigation Bruce, the team and I had conducted, was enough to convince the magistrate to commit the case against Baakza to full trial at the Old Bailey. A similar verdict was passed for Akbar.

Any trial would still be some months off but, for us, the workloads seemed to be ever-increasing. We were constantly getting statements, checking over documents for any damning evidence and preparing paperwork for our solicitors and the defence lawyers, because they had to have an opportunity to view all the relevant material. We had to schedule everything seized and reconcile it with statements from the team that recovered them. It became a real slog. I was reminded of something Bruce said to me, not long after I joined DFIB1: 'Investigation is 90 per cent office and 10 per cent fun.'

As the case proceeded to trial, however, there were changes within our team. Bruce's reward for his work on the operation, liaising with the Americans, was a promotion to senior investigating officer and a transfer to a VAT fraud team. Steve Berry took over as the senior case officer and, not long afterwards, we began to receive requests from the Bank of England to see documents. As BCCI's regulator, the evidence of corruption was highly damaging to them. It was clear the Bank of England were realising the BCCI was institutionally bent.

Another development at this time was that US Customs formally requested any evidence relating to Noriega's accounts.

Under the legislation, if you had reasonable suspicion of a drugs crime, you could get access to people's bank accounts, as long as you had a production order signed by a judge. We had identified further Noriega accounts at BCCI and now needed copies of these. Our standard procedure was to go to Southwark

Crown Court. Not only was it a five-minute walk across the bridge from Custom House, but we had a tame judge there who nearly always did our bidding.

Within Customs, there was various guidance on where best to take certain cases. For example, Southwark was the favoured court for fraud cases, because jurors there didn't like the idea of rich people fiddling their taxes or committing fraud. That was preferable to trying a fraud case out in the suburbs or county towns, where, let's just say, the jury might be less concerned, as perhaps some of them might be committing some form of their own low-level tax fraud. I was always told never do a drugs case in inner London, because, perhaps unfairly, it was suggested that half the jury would either be taking drugs themselves or sometimes have a connection to the trade, so would be sympathetic to any defendants.

Snaresbrook Crown Court was the most notorious. We were told never to take cases there because it was in east London and had the lowest conviction rate of any court in the country. The average conviction rate nationally was around 69 per cent, but in Snaresbrook it was as low as 42 per cent, the reason being that the east London electoral roll had a larger-than-average number of residents with criminal records.

Steve drafted the application for more of Noriega's bank accounts. Normally the format is to put 'Regina versus' the name of the suspect. As it was such a high-profile case it had to be kept secret, so Steve just put 'R versus N'.

Steve and I went over to Southwark Crown Court, expecting it to be a formality, but, for the first time, the judge refused. Clearly shaking when he saw the general's name, he gave the excuse that Noriega would have diplomatic immunity and wanted someone from the Foreign Office present before he would sign it. We had to go back with our lawyers and a bureaucratic mandarin from the Foreign Office before we got the production order signed.

From that moment on, Noriega became an official part of the inquiry. What had started out, from our perspective, as one transaction, had morphed into a huge investigation that threatened the very existence of BCCI and exposed the Bank of England's role as its regulator.

The US investigation showed that, even as early as the mid-eighties, the Bank of England had grave concerns about BCCI. Attempts had been made to get it to move out of London or move its registered office from the capital. However, its failure to act decisively would come back to haunt the regulator as the full scale of corruption was revealed.

By December 1989, as prosecutors prepared for trials on both sides of the Atlantic, the walls were closing in for Noriega. He had been clinging to power since May, after refusing to accept the result of the Panamanian national elections. Although an alliance of parties opposed to his dictatorship claimed their preferred candidate, Guillermo Endara, the winner, Noriega declared the election null and void, insisted he had won and blamed US-backed candidates in the opposition parties for causing irregularities in the results. As international tensions mounted, President Bush called on Noriega to honour the decision of the Panamanian electorate and relinquish his grip on power. The US put more pressure on Noriega's regime by stepping up its military presence at the canal.

Noriega also faced a coup from his own armed forces but foiled an attempt to unseat him by members of the Panamanian defence forces. As the future of the nation hung in the balance, President Bush branded Noriega a drug trafficker, and refused to negotiate with him. He denied having any previous knowledge of Noriega's involvement with the drug trade, despite their close ties while he was director of the CIA and the fact that he had been the chair of the task force on drugs while he served as vice president to Ronald Reagan.

On 15 December, the Panamanian general assembly declared a state of war with the USA, who responded by mounting an invasion. The USA said that, as well as safeguarding the lives of American citizens, defending democracy and protecting the integrity of long-standing treaties, it was combating drug trafficking. It branded Panama, under Noriega, a centre for money laundering and a transit point for trafficking to the US and Europe. The launch of Operation Just Cause saw US troops enter Panama, under President Bush's authorisation, to depose the country's leader.

Nearly 2,000 Panamanians died in the invasion, which lasted a month and resulted in the capture of Noriega, before his deportation and imprisonment in the US.

In January 1990, shortly before the trials of six key suspects from those arrested at the fake wedding got underway in Florida, BCCI agreed to a deal to plead guilty to US federal money laundering charges and pay $15 million, a record penalty against banks accused of handling drug money.

From its London headquarters, BCCI said the offences charged in the case were 'contrary to the expressed written policies' of the bank and were not known to senior management officials or its board of directors. The bank was put on five years' probation under the Federal Reserve System and agreed to open the books on Noriega to prosecutors.

At the trial against the money launderers in Tampa, Mazur gave evidence for eleven weeks, and as more details of C-Chase came to light, the attention to detail paid by Mazur throughout the operation was impressive. A reformed criminal he once met at a bail hearing advised him to use the US government funds paying for his investigation on expensive shoes, so he would give off a reassuring air of wealth if his cartel contacts ever caught a glimpse of his soles.

His team were supplied with Rolex watches to look the part on a trip to Zurich, and he also had use of a Cessna Citation jet and a 52-foot yacht in Miami, on which to entertain their new business partners. It was a far cry from the resources at our disposal.

In all, there had been 102 bank deposits of drug cash over the two years of the operation. They totalled $33,033,103. Of that total, $19,294,822 had been laundered by transfers through various branches of BCCI, from Panama to Geneva, Paris to London and Nassau.

The case shone a light on the scale of the problem, with the United Nations estimating that laundered money represented between 2 and 5 per cent of global GDP, making the black market the fifth-largest economy in the world. A fifth of all notes in circulation in the UK had traces of cocaine on them, it was claimed.

After six months of testimony in the precedent-setting case, all five of the international BCCI bankers and the one Colombian businessman arrested in Tampa were found guilty of scheming to launder $14 million in cocaine profits for the Medellín cartel. The jury deliberated for seven days before delivering its verdict.

Convicted of conspiracy and various counts of money laundering were Amjad Awan, Noriega's personal banker, Akbar Bilgrami of BCCI's Miami branch, Ian Howard and

Sibte Hassan of BCCI's Paris branch, Syed Aftab Hussain, who worked for BCCI in Panama, and Rudolf Armbrecht, a Colombian businessman. It was the first time international bankers had been convicted under US money laundering laws.

During the deliberations, one juror was dismissed for calling a reputed member of the Medellín cocaine cartel, using a telephone number he found in defendant Rudolf Armbrecht's address book.

The defendants were sentenced four months later, in November 1990. Judge Terrell Hodges sentenced Awan to twelve years in prison and a $100,000 fine; Bilgrami to twelve years; Hussain to seven years; Howard to five years and Hassan to three years in jail. Armbrecht received the longest sentence of twelve years and nine months.

In between the verdict and sentencing, Mazur was back in London for the trial of Asif Baakza at the Old Bailey. His ordeal was considerably lighter than the international bankers, spending two days on the witness stand.

Despite my reservations, the Customs agent's evidence held up in the face of cross examination and Baakza's defence was not able to convince the jury he was an unwitting fall guy. The jury found him guilty and the judge, who had a habit of falling asleep after lunch, sentenced him to one year in prison. The maximum sentence was fourteen years imprisonment. Did the judge share my unease that this case was a stitch-up?

A few weeks later, Ziauddin Akbar was also found guilty and sentenced to eighteen months in jail.

With Awan facing a long stretch inside, Mazur and his Customs negotiators tried to get him to do a deal in return for the details of Noriega's secret accounts. In the raft of documents seized from Capcom it was shown that $23 million of Noriega's fortune was moved from BCCI, but the investigators needed inside knowledge to help establish the precise details.

Awan had knowledge of tens of millions of dollars that had arrived at the Panama City BCCI branch in suitcases. Those cases, which Awan picked up directly from Noriega, or his officers in the Panamanian Defence Forces, delivered as much as $3.4 million at a time.

Awan's testimony became the basis for a second indictment against Ziauddin and further cases against his former bosses at BCCI, including bank president Swaleh Naqvi. However, the Home Office bungled Syed Ziauddin Ali Akbar's extradition to the US on corruption charges, with the High Court ruling they had spent too long awaiting extradition since his arrest in September last year.

The problem had begun when Akbar was released on parole in 1991, halfway through his eighteen-month sentence, and fled to France, which later extradited him to Britain to face the BCCI charges. The US had wanted him extradited to face a charge that he had accepted a $15-million bribe from BCCI for not disclosing details of corruption to a US senator, but the French authorities blocked the move because they had only agreed to his extradition to Britain on money laundering charges. A lengthy exchange over procedural points then took place between the two countries.

One person who did eventually make it to the US to stand trial was Nazir Chinoy. Faced with the prospect of suffering a similar fate to the other defendants, Chinoy decided to talk. And what a story he told.

The former head of BCCI's French and African operations testified before a Senate subcommittee that the bank's Pakistan office regularly arranged for teenage girls to be brought in from the countryside to 'take care of any personal needs' of their wealthy Middle Eastern clients.

Chinoy confirmed that girls aged from fifteen to seventeen were procured as prostitutes, although in Pakistan they were referred to as 'singing and dancing girls'. He revealed that providing prostitutes for BCCI customers was handled by the 'protocol department', where the primary responsibility was to look after wealthy clients and their families when they visited Pakistan. The department spent about $6 million, employed about 450 people in 1988, including 100 chauffeurs and numerous gardeners and cooks, in addition to the young girls, he said.

Testifying, Chinoy named a woman whose job it was to bring girls in from the countryside. The girls were often taken in groups of 60 to department stores, where jewellery and clothes were bought for them. Rahim went on to become the interior decorator for the ruler of Abu Dhabi, Sheikh Zayed al-Nahyan.

Chinoy pleaded guilty to laundering drug money and said other forms of corruption, including the bribery of foreign officials, tax evasion and loans for arms sales to Iran, were systemic at the bank.

He named Sani Ahmad as the head of the BCCI protocol department. Ahmad later came to Washington to head the BCCI office, where his job was to contact and entertain embassy personnel and officials of such organisations as the World Bank and the International Monetary Fund. The testimony led to Ahmad's later arrest for questioning by the US authorities.

Chinoy also said Adnan Khashoggi, the Saudi arms dealer, wrote cheques on a BCCI Monte Carlo branch, even though he didn't have enough funds to cover the cheques. Khashoggi deposited the cheques in London bank accounts as a way of advancing funds to cover arms sales to Iran. Chinoy said there were about nine transactions totalling $16 million arranged like that.

Testimonies from Awan, Chinoy, Bilgrami and other bankers prompted new investigations against the entire BCCI board, and a US Senate subcommittee on terrorism, narcotics and international operations held an inquiry into the bank, chaired by John Kerry.

With probably no other option, BCCI pleaded guilty to federal racketeering charges and a New York State indictment, agreeing to forfeit its $550 million in US assets, to pay a $200 million fine to the Federal Reserve and break up its international business.

On 5 July 1991, the Bank of England finally acted on the material we had seized and what, by then, were regular reports in places like *Private Eye*, of 'massive and widespread fraud' linked to money laundering at BCCI, or the 'Bank of Crooks and Cocaine International' as it was becoming known colloquially.

When the regulator pulled the plug on the corrupt bank, BCCI losses were discovered to have mounted to $12 billion. On the day it went out of business there were reports that outgoing employees at branches in London were grabbing huge wads of cash from the tills.

Aside from the international investors caught up in the scandal there were some unlikely victims from the bank's closure. For instance, a tiny Western Isles council in Scotland lost more than £23 million in the wake of the collapse. Incredibly, it deposited money right to the end, paying in the last £1 million on the day it went bust.

Other UK councils also lost money but none on the scale of the Western Isles. The local authority was only saved by a little-known government device called the Special Islands Needs Allowance, which allowed £3 million to be diverted to the council without the government having to compensate other local authorities which had lost money.

For a year spanning 1991 and 1992, an inquiry was held into the bank's collapse, led by Lord Bingham. In his report, he criticised the Bank of England's regulation of BCCI as 'a tragedy of errors, misunderstandings and failures of communication'. The bank, he said, had ignored repeated warnings before BCCI's demise and had shown a 'marked lack of curiosity'.

Senator John Kerry's report to the foreign relations committee delivered his verdict that 'BCCI's criminality included fraud by BCCI and BCCI customers involving billions of dollars; money laundering in Europe, Africa, Asia, and the Americas; BCCI's bribery of officials in most of those locations; support of terrorism, arms trafficking, and the sale of nuclear technologies; management of prostitution; the commission and facilitation of income tax evasion, smuggling, and illegal immigration; illicit purchases of banks and real estate; and a panoply of financial crimes limited only by the imagination of its officers and customers.'

It took a further 21 years and $656 million of fees paid to two firms of lawyers and accountants before the files were finally closed on the BCCI banking scandal in 2012. By then its collapse was estimated to have totalled $20 billion.

Liquidators from Deloitte and lawyers from Hogan Lovells explained how the quest for recoveries had taken them around the world, to 'deserted warehouses' and remote locations, where documents were found rotting in damp, humid and rat-infested rooms. On some occasions the inspection of papers was only permitted under armed guard. Deloitte amassed a library of 95,000 box files, containing about 100 million chaotically ordered documents.

The failure of BCCI revealed a scale of corruption, money laundering and other secretive activities never seen before. As suspected, organisations from the CIA to mujahideen guerrillas were all linked to BCCI.

In all, there were more than 60 prosecutions. In the UK, Abbas Gokal, a businessman with ties to the bank, received the longest sentence, a record fourteen-year jail term.

For Steve, the continuing investigation meant he was often required to travel to Florida for hearings relating to the Noriega case. But, in terms of DFIB1, with Bruce away to another department and the Baakza case progressing to a full trial, our work on Operation C-Chase was coming to an end. By the time our banker, Tango One, came to trial, I was away working on other things. I was relieved to be getting away from the drudgery of having to sift through and organise the mountain of paperwork. BCCI was a case so toxic it was almost impossible not to feel poisoned by it, no matter how involved you were in the investigation.

But the success of C-Chase and Robert Mazur's operation had a big influence on the UK Customs' elite money laundering team. Colleagues had an early setback trying to confiscate £3-million worth of assets from a convicted cannabis smuggler who, after being found guilty, was asked to account for his wealth with no legitimate income. 'I'm a bank robber,' he testified, so the judge did not then have the power to make an order seizing his crime-related assets.

That case aside, after seeing what could be achieved by setting up an undercover investigation, we decided the best course of action was to try to emulate it ourselves. As they say, set a thief to catch a thief. We were going into the drugs money laundering business.

CHAPTER 11

The old boys' network

Its presence at first raised few eyebrows. What was special about yet another financial services office in the City of London?

It was a small operation but the advice it offered was sound. One of the two full-time members of staff was exactly what you'd expect to find in such an office. He looked like a banker and talked like one. This was hardly surprising; after all, he was ex-Barclays. He knew the system inside out, and he was particularly well-versed in the loopholes. His colleague also had extensive experience in financial services, but he had more of the air of an east-London street hustler than a corporate office manager. He talked the language of their target clientele. They were an ideal fit.

Another advantage this business had over the banks was their apparent discretion. In the current climate, where the established banks were getting a reputation for informing on customers, criminals couldn't be too careful. Word started to spread that this financial advice office was the place to go for expert advice to clean some dirty cash.

If only the criminals knew that this little enterprise was the latest Customs trick in the fight against money launderers. The success of C-Chase had got the Customs hierarchy thinking.

What better way to collect intelligence on would-be money launderers than to pose as one? And so, Customs set up a front company, rented an office and opened for business. The two men staffing this bespoke service were both newly recruited undercover officers.

Since I joined the Investigation Division there had been a change of policy regarding recruitment. Put bluntly, they were struggling to find decent people and, as the division expanded and experienced officers left the service, there was a dearth of talent coming through. Where previously you had to have worked in one of the other divisions before being able to apply to be an investigator, now you could apply directly from the general civilian labour market.

Not that finding willing applicants was hard. Customs cases generated reams of positive coverage in the national press and, following on from the success of *The Collectors* and *The Duty Men*, there were further documentaries glamorising the work of the unique service. Once vacancies were thrown open to all and sundry, the ID was inundated with applications. When people saw the remit of our powers, it was an easy sell. It was particularly appealing to bored office workers, ex-bankers and former military personnel. The general rule was that anyone from the Armed Forces was sent to the operational drugs teams, those with a financial background went to DFIB and if they came from any other walk of life they were recommended for the Customs fraud or VAT teams.

Once these two new recruits were trained up, Customs set them up in the City and investigators put the word out on the street through their informants that here was a company that would wash drugs money discreetly.

The office was not part of our team, but we helped whenever

needed. When known drug smugglers fell for the bait and arranged a meeting with the officers, we went along to help with intelligence gathering and to provide added security.

Investigators on the drugs teams ran two types of informants – cooperating informants (CIs) and participating inform-ants (PIs). Cooperating informants provided detailed tip-offs, while participating informants were actively involved in the importation or other crimes.

As C-Chase had demonstrated, and our cases so far had largely shown, the only way we had a realistic chance of secur-ing a conviction and confiscating assets was if we had the evidence and testimony of an undercover officer or an inform-ant with a death wish.

While the covert office had some success in gathering intel-ligence, in practice, it wasn't the ideal tool to secure evidence. If they had turned around and started arresting people who used the service, the office was finished. Word would get out and no one would dare use it. But, while it didn't necessarily produce cases that could be prosecuted, it enticed people about whom we previously had no intelligence.

Its popularity also highlighted that, following the anti-money laundering legislation, criminals understood that dodgy financial transactions were now being monitored by the banks. They were looking for alternative routes to launder money and that meant moving away from regulated institutions to deregu-lated ones.

One surprising outlet that criminals were taking full advantage of was a service that had branches all over the UK, where they could move large sums of money in a range of currencies with no questions asked. It was bureaux de change.

Only when Customs started looking into this sector did the scale of the problem become apparent. Bureaux were estimated to move more money than the City of London every week.

One of the drugs teams received specific intelligence about a bureau near Victoria Station, where several of the biggest London smugglers moved millions every day. Word was getting around that this was a good way to get rid of dirty cash.

We helped with the surveillance, discreetly watching the bureau, monitoring who came and went. We noted all vehicle registrations and made a breakthrough when several of them matched with known heroin importers. One family operated out of Stratford, and we spotted a Mercedes belonging to the kingpin making regular visits to the bureau. It was the proof of the link the team needed and it led to arrests of several family members.

By this time, we had changed our surveillance techniques. Rather than having four cars following a target vehicle, we adopted tactics favoured by MI5 and the military in Northern Ireland. Those same four cars created a box around the target, with no one car directly behind. At a junction the three cars ahead of the target each picked a different route. Depending on which route the target took, the cars would manoeuvre around to switch positions and reform the box. If the target became stationary, footmen were put out to follow on the street. It was considered a more reliable system and it was recognition that criminals were getting very savvy.

We couldn't help but notice that the people we targeted on the drug side nearly always had a minder vehicle; the target was rarely on its own. An added complication was when the minder vehicle was a motorbike, which was far nimbler in heavy traffic and able to identify any unusual movements quicker.

Some of the lengths criminals went to to avoid detection were quite impressive. We saw a target drive to a motorway service station, park their car, then walk over the bridge to collect another vehicle on the other side in which to drive off in the opposite direction. Some service stations had staff-only bridges the public couldn't use and the crooks would just drive across, knowing it was unlikely they could be followed.

Other targets created rural pinch points, where they would pass an accomplice watching the road from a phone box, jotting down the registrations and models of any car following behind. When the target car doubled back they would know if any of the previous vehicles were still following.

In the late 1990s, payphones were considered safer means of communications than analogue mobile phones or landlines, but Alpha were still able to tap in and listen to payphones if they had right the number. However, certain criminals grew wise to this. One smuggler used to use a different pay phone for every conversation, even driving to one 30 miles away in the hope they wouldn't be listened in on.

One trick we had to counter this, though, was to watch the call being made and, when the call box was vacated, jump in, and hit the last number dialled button. It almost always gave us another number to go on.

❘❘❘

As if to remind me of my standing within DFIB, I was put in charge of what we affectionately termed 'the crazies' – the phone calls we received from cranks, time-wasters and downright lunatics. Someone was always designated to take them.

It used to be Steve's responsibility, but after Bruce left he grew sick of handling the calls, along with everything else he had to look after, so passed them on to me.

I took one call from a member of the public, who was convinced the Mafia was laundering money through a council in south Wales. We had been fobbing him off for a while but one day he turned up at Custom House with cuttings from his local paper as proof of his allegations. He wanted us to launch our own investigation. We politely told him it was a matter for the local Collection Investigation Unit.

Another was from the police in Portsmouth. They were having trouble with a retired Customs officer who was finding it impossible to give up the day job. He had kept hold of his uniform and, even though he no longer worked for the service, was still standing on the High Street, stopping cars that had come off the ferry. He announced to baffled drivers that he was Customs control and he needed to inspect their vehicles, looking for drugs. He would cause a three-mile tailback to the docks. I'd have to placate some weary copper, who'd call, saying: 'He's back again.' It was a sad story, really, so we tried to appeal to the local collection to see if they could assist him.

One call that was passed on to me, however, was to have a significant impact. There was a delightful voice on the end of the phone with an intriguing name, one of Cleopatra's handmaidens. Charmian Gooch called from the Environmental Investigation Agency (EIA). They were ex-Greenpeace activists, who set up an organisation to conduct undercover operations looking at eco-crime. They were specifically concerned with wildlife trafficking and the illegal trade in African ivory. In the wake of the furore over BCCI, they had information that the bank had been helping to facilitate money laundering from elephant poaching. Their office was in Islington and so, on my way home to Tottenham one night, I went round to see them.

Charmian was full of energy and desire to bring an end to animal exploitation and was keen to know if we had uncovered any evidence into illegal wildlife trade during our search of BCCI documents. I had to explain that the remit of our search was very narrow, but I referred her to Customs at Heathrow, which had a very successful wildlife unit, to see if they could help. I might not have been able to give her the answers she was looking for, but we remained in contact.

|||

While the recruitment for Customs investigators was broadening, the only team that didn't recruit externally was Alpha. It continued to hand-pick the best candidates from the investigations service. It was considered an honour to be selected. However, with this policy, it struggled for recruits from ethnic-minority backgrounds, which meant many foreign smuggling organisations were difficult to target because they couldn't translate what was being said on the calls.

Customs didn't always get the selection process right in their recruitment. One of our new colleagues transferred in had quite a chequered history. Alex Wright was ex-Alpha and a senior officer. Someone with that experience would normally have been considered an asset to any team. He was an amiable, intelligent chap and certainly a very capable investigator, but word soon got round about the reason for his departure from Alpha.

During an inquiry into cocaine smugglers, the name of a well-known TV personality kept cropping up. She was in her mid-twenties and already enjoying a glittering career, but she was clearly a regular user, and perhaps even a small supplier to her extensive network of showbiz contacts. She was part of a very famous family, and her connections stretched from pop culture to cinema and even Westminster. Rather than leave any follow-up investigation to the relevant drugs team, Alex contacted the celebrity directly, and the details are unclear but either used the personal information he'd gleaned from the bugged calls to ask her out, or, even worse, blackmailed her into seeing him.

Either way, his bosses at Alpha found out about it. Rather than kick him out of Customs completely and subject him to the full force of the law, they quietly moved him to our team. The last thing they wanted was any negative publicity surrounding the Investigation Division. Anything negative was better kept in house. Who wanted their dirty laundry washed in public, when that might draw unwelcome attention to the remit of the telephone intercepts? The unsavoury case showed that unless Alpha officers were closely monitored there was always a temptation to misuse the information they came across. Ultimately there needed to be greater oversight.

Alex didn't stay with us for long and he soon moved to Bermuda to work on the anti-money laundering team out there. When he told me he got the job, he said: 'How quickly they forget.'

| | |

Customs might have been throwing open its doors but that didn't necessarily mean anyone could apply – or expect to be treated equally. The service was still very much an old boys' network. This was demonstrated to me when I inquired about a new posting in Miami, which I thought sounded exciting. I pictured myself being a Don-Johnson type out there, enjoying a glamorous lifestyle and working in one of the biggest drug hotspots in the world, with boats coming in all the time from South America, via islands that Escobar's empire had bought. It was also the location for the biggest CIA outstation in the world, with the perceived threat from Cuba on its doorstep. I felt it was an ideal opportunity for someone like me, who had anti-money laundering experience, but it went to a drug liaison officer based in South America. I was told by one senior investigator that my interest in the position didn't progress because I 'didn't run with the buffalos'.

I asked Steve what that meant. He told me it would become clear at the next annual dinner we held for the entire Investigation Division at the Connaught Rooms in Holborn. It was one of the highlights of the year – a full dinner and piss-up we paid for ourselves – featuring a live band made up of officers, who sang songs poking fun at the hierarchy or the big events over the last twelve months. One example was after the Matrix Churchill affair. The Coventry-based engineering firm faced a Customs trial after allegedly breaching export controls by selling arms to Saddam Hussein. The trial collapsed, following Tory minister Alan Clark's admission that he had been 'economical with the *actualité*' regarding what he knew about export licenses to Iraq. In its wake, the band sang a hilarious song about the scandal, which included the lines:

'Don't go shipping out weaponry,
Without anyone else but me,
It's the *actualité*.'

The dinner was always held in the Connaught Rooms, even though there were always moans about the poor-quality food.

When the next one came around, I reminded Steve what he'd said and asked him why we always went there.

'Have you seen what's next door?' he asked.

I hadn't realised – it was Freemasons Hall, their UK headquarters.

'It's next to the grand lodge,' Steve said. 'This is the mason's catering unit. And look at the grand poobah up there ...'

He was referring to Derek Henderson, the over-promoted Mancunian SIO. As usual, he was lording it over the proceedings, which normally attracted a high-profile guest of honour, like a member of the Met Police's top brass. Henderson always gave the keynote speech in front of the Customs chair, the Treasury bigwigs and the Chief Investigation Officer.

'Is he a mason, too?' I said.

Steve shrugged. 'What do you think?'

Henderson certainly loved the apparent prestige that came with his position among the team, but he also had the ignominy of being in charge of the Custom House bar – when it was caught out for not paying VAT!

The bar had enjoyed VAT-free status for decades, during the time when Custom House was run by the London Port Collection. It was one of the perks of DFIB being the only ID team moved there. We used to drink with the local guys most nights after work. When Customs kicked out London Port and moved all the investigators over from New Fetter Lane, it became the ID bar.

Suddenly, we got a pack from Stratford VAT office, part of the London Port collection, asking if we'd registered. It was the same one sent to any business making more than £20,000 a year. Clearly the local collection did it to spite us. Whether he had masonic connections or not, Henderson had no choice but to register the bar and pay VAT like everyone else.

Geoff Heslop, our ACIO, had also apparently just joined the masons, which was seen as a good career move. I couldn't believe such an ancient order still held influence over a service that was apparently trying to modernise. That was obviously just lip-service, however; the old prejudices remained, and there was always an undercurrent of discrimination.

|||

In spring 1990, not long before the trial of Asif Baakza was due to get underway, an internal reshuffle across the four DFIB teams saw me move away from the Uniforms. I was only moving to the next office, but I was joining Drugs W, or the Whiskies. Although I felt some sadness at leaving the Uniforms, there was also relief that I was leaving a lot of the monotonous C-Chase work behind. The Whiskies were another anti-money laundering team, but they were more concerned with seizing financial assets of heroin traffickers, and were largely office-based. I hoped it would reignite my interest in the ID and remind me of why I wanted to join them in the first place.

CHAPTER 12

‖‖

On the Whiskies

W e'd looked in every room. There was nothing. Not a sniff of cash. No computer, no files, no biscuit tins full of notes. It was like she knew we were coming. I had been warned that this was how it would be.

'You never find anything,' Jack Burns told me. He was referring to Asian drug smugglers. 'They're too good for that.'

While white, British, men involved in the drug trade couldn't help revealing the spoils of their successes – splashing out on a new house, flash car, huge TVs or walking around dripping in gold – the importers with connections in India or Pakistan were far more discreet. Whether they sent it all back *hawala*-style or lived frugally to remain below the radar and were just better at hiding large amounts of cash, it was a known fact that you rarely recovered any assets during a search of their property.

That didn't stop us doing them though, which was why I was in Blackburn on a rain-soaked morning in spring 1990. It was my first case for the Whiskies. For a team that spent most of its time indoors, this was encouraging. We were out of London, helping Manchester ID out on a heroin case.

They had seized a shipment and arrested a gang of smugglers who were bringing a sizeable amount into Manchester nearly every month, on Pakistan International Airline flights. We helped on the house searches.

It didn't take us long to go through the modest terraced two-up, two-down house. The smuggler's wife hadn't been happy to see us, but she had been calm throughout our search. Did she know we were wasting our time?

I'd finished searching the last bedroom when I spotted a door at the end of the landing. It was an airing cupboard, and some clothes were draped over a shelf. I don't know whether it was the thought that they wouldn't dry piled like that, or some other intuition, but I lifted the clothes to find a Tesco shopping bag underneath. I opened it. Inside were banknotes. Hundreds of them, neatly bundled.

'Found something,' I called to the rest of the team.

Jack Burns appeared.

'Nice one,' he said, peering in. 'Look.'

He pulled out one of the bundles. The notes all looked well used but counted as though by a bank teller. The note on top was marked Bank of Scotland.

'Shows how far he distributed his gear,' Jack said. 'It's amazing how often we see that. Even when there's no connection north of the border, we usually end up seeing Scottish money.'

We concluded our search and as we left the house, I saw the wife's face looked a lot more disgruntled. When the haul was later counted, we discovered there was £10,000 stashed in that bag. They'd have a hard time arguing that was earned legitimately. At crown court, the gang were all convicted of drug trafficking offences – especially after we'd waved the bags of seized cash and photographs of it inside the airing cupboard under the jury's wide and covetous eyes.

My new job involved preparing financial statements

identifying convicts' assets, bank accounts, legitimate incomes and liabilities. We would then have a hearing and invite the judge to formally seize any assets by making a Confiscation Order. For this case, I'd prepared a full financial statement and we checked their bank accounts, property and anything else we could find, which wasn't much for a medium-sized heroin smuggler, the only trace of wealth was that bag of cash. Even their house was rented. It was considered a success though – and a decent start to my time on Drugs W, who had been struggling for victories for a while.

My move to the team had been a complete surprise. One morning Walt came to see me and said: 'From Monday, you are joining Whisky.'

I later found they were shuffling people around the whole branch. Jack Burns was moving with me to be one of the Whiskies' senior officers, which I was quite happy about as we got on well, and I'd got to know people across the branch over the past couple of years, so it wasn't all new faces.

The SIO there was Ian Stewart, who'd led the search for Noriega evidence at the BCCI. He was a big, crazy Scottish guy, who I was reminded of years later when I saw the actor Brendan Gleeson, if he wore lashings of Brylcreem, like Stewart always did. While softly spoken, he had the character to match his massive build and fiery eyes. I had a lot of time for him but, while he stood at your desk regaling you with tales of his time in the army, he had a habit of slipping his hand down his trousers and scratching his balls, which annoyed everyone, not least of all my fellow junior officer, Carrie Daniels, who recoiled in disgust every time he came near. His personal hygiene also left little to be desired, and he'd regularly scratch his back against the big office cupboards.

Our other senior officer was Jerry Kidson, who I got on well with, largely because he was a Yorkshireman, from Hull. But he had a terrible temper and was nicknamed Upminster, which was 'way past Barking on the District Line'. A techy colleague once corrupted his office phone, so it added '5' to any number dialled. After a week of this, it crashed straight through the office window. He was mad, but looked like George Clooney, so was a favourite of many female colleagues.

Branch 16 was split between Drugs Victor, which did cannabis and cocaine confiscation cases, and Whisky, which focused on heroin proceeds. We weren't an operational team but helped the other teams out when called upon, usually only on the money side, which drugs teams neither understood nor were generally interested in. As I'd been warned, I quickly discovered that our work could often be fruitless, hunting for assets among the *hawala* operators who lived in small houses in rundown inner-city areas and drove second-hand Skodas.

I didn't have to worry too much about that in the short-term, however, because after a few weeks I learned a place had come up on a police advanced driving course, something all investigators needed to attend for future surveillance work.

It was May 1990 and by then I was no longer with the detective I had been going out with from Bishopsgate, but was seeing a girl in Sheffield, a friend of an old colleague in the VAT office. This meant that on Friday nights, after finishing work, I headed up the M1 to see her. One night, while travelling through Derbyshire on deserted roads, I got up to 100 miles per hour. That's when I caught sight of the blue lights in my mirror.

By coincidence, the driving course was held at Derbyshire Police headquarters in Ripley. When I turned up on the Monday to start the course, the first thing the police instructors asked for was everyone's driving licence.

'I haven't got mine,' I said.

'Where is it?'

'It's downstairs with your traffic department being annotated with three points and attached to a fine notice.'

It was an inauspicious start, particularly because the instructors saw it as their role to break us. Certainly, they were keen to rid us of our bad habits. As I'd only been driving for a relatively short time, I didn't have that many – aside from an over-eager right foot.

The instructors were all hard-bitten traffic cops who'd seen everything on the road, multiple pile-ups and carnage. They tried to intimidate us, but the chief instructor quickly realised he couldn't faze me.

'You're so laid back you should be in the fucking boot,' he said.

I just smiled.

Over the four-week course we covered theory as well as practice. One of the key skills was learning to drive with minimal braking, especially on motorways. If you're always on the brake you increase your chances of skidding. We were taught instead to look a long distance ahead of what's in front and to use the accelerator to reduce speed. They taught double de-clutching, which is when, rather than putting in the clutch and changing gear, you go first into neutral, then hit the accelerator to match the new gear speed, then change. It was a tricky operation to master, because you had to gauge the speed of the car and how much acceleration you would need, but it was meant to make for smoother gear changes and inject greater power when needed, say, for overtaking.

Another bit of advice was to drive to the rev count and not to the clock. They taught us how to drive out of a skid, which was to come off the brakes, straighten up and hit the accelerator. To put this into practice, they let us loose on a skid pan in a big lorry.

All eventualities were catered for. The most frightening aspect was overtaking on blind bends on country roads. Their procedure was to make sure you had an escape route, like an entrance to a farmer's field, but it was pretty hairy in practice. They took us through the Peak District, driving high-performance, police-spec three-litre cars. Ultimately, the goal was to teach us to be able to drive fast, but safely, and keep as low a gear as possible for maximum acceleration.

Once, when we were out on the M67 near Manchester, the car in front of mine contained three Customs officers and a police trainer. Everything was fine until suddenly they skidded off the motorway and somersaulted down a bank. The car had hit a patch of oil. Fortunately, they all had their seat belts on and they all walked away relatively unhurt, but it was a terrifying reminder of how quickly things can change when you're driving at high speed.

At the end of the course, we sat a theory test before the practical, which involved driving on the M1 in an unmarked police car. We had to drive at 150 miles per hour and we weren't allowed to touch our brake. Doing so would result in failing the course.

Behind the wheel of an unmarked 4.2-litre Jaguar, I had to prove I could handle such a car at top speed, so I pushed it to 150 miles per hour, in the fast lane, clearing people out in front by flashing with my front lights. It was tremendous fun and, although we weren't remotely in the same league as the police officers, I think we earned their respect.

I was delighted to pass and almost immediately I had to put my newfound skills to use. I was with Jack on surveillance, and we were hurtling down an A road in the middle of nowhere. I was doing close to 130 miles per hour when suddenly the car skidded. We were heading for a farmer's field, but I adopted the technique I'd learnt, straightening the car, then gently hitting the gas. I didn't touch the brake. Do that, and you're dead.

|||

The case where I tested my new-found skills didn't amount to anything, but another the team was working on was coming to court. The Whiskies had helped an operational drugs team on an unusual heroin case. A smuggler from India had been bringing in a kilo of the stuff at a time, disguised as onion powder. As a ruse, it was clever, because it was a product regularly imported from that part of the world for food preparation. The couriers he used had no idea what they were carrying, and the organisers thought the smell put off the sniffer dogs.

Incidentally, in our experience, the idea that specially trained drug dogs could sniff out narcotics, was nonsense. Often they were used as an excuse to search someone already under suspicion. An officer on the Romeos (Drugs R), which looked after cocaine, and was the team I'd watched on the TV documentary, told me they had intelligence on couriers who were suspected of smuggling some of Colombia's finest in Samsonite suitcases through airports. The tip came from Alpha and, as usual, they didn't want to give away any clues as to the source of the information and wanted the interception of the couriers to look like it was random. The plan was to put a sniffer dog on the suspect suitcase in the hope it would pick up the scent, giving them a reason to open it up. Nine times out of ten, the officer said, the dog didn't work. He said they had to nudge the dog to make it yelp and claimed that was the signal it had found something.

In the case of the onion powder, the dogs weren't needed because the intelligence had come through an informant. An unwitting courier had put the heroin on his kitchen shelf, believing it to be the actual powder.

Jerry Kidson worked the case, aided by a recently recruited officer from Glasgow. Alan Murray was a big, shy, dour guy, possibly because he commuted 400 miles back to his home city every Friday, as his wife was pregnant. He was a nice guy, however, and very dedicated, and he and Jerry worked wonders on the case.

The smuggler had been convicted and Jerry went after his wife for money laundering, as she was moving cash while her husband was in prison. The rest of us helped, with surveillance, checking bank accounts, searching the woman's house. It was a complex case, and although Jerry had enough to take it to court, it was going to be hard to convince a jury of her guilt.

One thing we did have in our favour was our crown counsel, Derek Spencer, the silk the Solicitors' Office chose to represent the Crown. Derek was quite the character, very formal and droll, an archetypal patrician Tory, which was perhaps not surprising, given he was a Conservative MP and went on to be Solicitor General.

When the smuggler's wife came to trial, her defence played up the cultural differences, arguing that she didn't do anything without her husband's orders. A key witness for them was a female university professor, who spent two days on the stand as an expert trying to convince the jury that no Indian woman would do anything without her husband's say-so and, therefore, the defendant shouldn't be found guilty. From the faces of the jury, it looked like they were buying the story.

It wasn't looking good, but then it was time for Derek to begin his cross-examination of the expert witness. He got up and said: 'Could you tell me the name of the Indian prime minister from 1980 to 1984 please?'

'Indira Gandhi,' the professor replied.

'Thank you. No further questions,' Derek said and sat down.

That single question – clearly illustrating that if a woman could become prime minister it wasn't that much of a cultural problem – destroyed two days of evidence in ten seconds and turned the case in our favour. It was brilliant.

The jury convicted her and the judge sentenced her to seven years, which was a remarkable result for Jerry. I wasn't in court but Jack, who filled me in on the details, said he had never seen anything like it.

|||

Intriguing cases were coming up all the time on the Whiskies. The Golfs – the target team Drugs G – needed our help while investigating a heroin smuggler from Pakistan. In every source country, Customs had a drug liaison officer (DLO). The DLO there was trying to set up a buy, using a participating inform-ant (PI). The exporter Bashir Uddin Peracha had been sending massive amounts by post to contacts in the UK but would never set foot on British soil. To set up the deal they hoped would flush him out, they arranged for an undercover officer to pose as a buyer, and they came to us to help facilitate the payment.

Jack and I went to one of our banking contacts to organise a banker's draft for £250,000. Once arranged, the Golfs lured the smuggler to Cyprus on the pretence that that was where he would meet the buyer and receive his money. The Golf's undercover officer was based in the UK, a real Cockney, and the perfect guy to carry out a controlled delivery, the name given to importations carried out with the knowledge and supervision of Customs.

Although Cyprus ceased to be a crown colony in 1960, when it became independent, Britain retained two large military bases. One of these was the Dhekelia Cantonment, on the eastern side of the island, on the border with the Turkish-controlled northern territory of Cyprus.

Peracha was wary of travelling to a country from where he could be extradited, so insisted on only meeting on the Turkish side. The Customs officers agreed to the smuggler's request and invited him to a restaurant near Famagusta, where he would receive his money.

Working with the British Army, the Golfs dismantled the border crossing at Dhekelia, removing all military signs and flags. Amazingly, they also convinced the Turkish Army to remove their soldiers from the crossing. The Golfs met with Peracha and told him they were taking him to the restaurant. Instead, under the cover of darkness, they drove him over the border onto British sovereign territory at Dhekelia, without Peracha realising. The Golfs again went to great lengths to make sure it didn't look like a military site. They took all the signs down and transformed the officers' mess into an ordinary restaurant.

Once they had Peracha safely on British territory, they arrested him. To fly him back to the UK meant taking him to Episkopi, on the western side of the island, but if they moved him by road it would mean entering Cypriot jurisdiction. Instead, they put him in a helicopter and flew him over international waters to the other base, then transported him back to the UK to stand trial. It was a staggeringly audacious plot – perfectly executed.

Peracha claimed he had been kidnapped. He had a point. It was extraordinary rendition, long before the Iraq War. He later stood trial at Knightsbridge Crown Court, where he was convicted of smuggling heroin and jailed for twenty years.

Interestingly, there was another drug connection to Turkish-controlled Northern Cyprus. Henry told me Asil Nadir, the chief executive of Polly Peck, who fled the UK in 1990 when facing charges over the collapse of the former textile-company-turned-top-FTSE-100 firm, was not only one of the country's biggest fraudsters, but also a big-time heroin smuggler.

Nadir, a British Turkish Cypriot, was a fugitive on the island for seventeen years, before returning to the UK in 2010, where he was ultimately found guilty of ten counts of theft totalling £29 million and sentenced to ten years in prison.

As Henry said, anyone who suddenly experienced a dramatic change in fortunes was nearly always up to no good. So it proved in Nadir's case.

Controlled deliveries were a risky strategy but, in terms of evidence and intelligence, they were effective tools when it came to snaring smugglers. We would pay the traffickers in Asia for the intelligence of what drugs were on which plane. Customs officers would be monitoring the consignment all the way from India or Pakistan to Heathrow. Once it reached the UK, we had to make the decision whether to let the drugs run live or switch them for a substitute package. Letting the consignment run could lead us to a warehouse or home address and to finding out who the distributors were in the UK. This was highly controversial, however, because if we lost the shipment we were screwed. The practice was fraught with difficulties and didn't always go to plan. And, because they nearly always involved big money, any failures were costly to the Treasury.

I was told of one case where a DLO in Asia used a PI to set up a controlled delivery to import heroin to the UK. A massive reward payment for £250,000 was authorised. The money was passed to the informant, but the deal didn't come off. The PI stole the cash and disappeared. It comes with the territory, after all. We were dealing with ruthless criminals. Often the informants were rival smugglers, keen to see a competitor removed from the market.

There was another situation when colleague Jack Dodds transferred to Pakistan to be the DLO there. He was working with informants and for some reason crossed the border, without backup, into Afghanistan. Every DLO had a desk officer in Custom House. Word came through his desk officer that Jack had been kidnapped and was being held in a cave. Everybody in the ID was shocked, but there was also consternation that he had put himself in that position. The story made the national press and it ran for a few weeks before some international diplomacy eventually freed him. We took that to mean a ransom had been paid, although that would never be confirmed officially.

|||

The Whiskies helped several operational drugs teams. Drugs F, or the Foxtrots, dealt with Iranians and people that fell under identification code one, which meant white people, or Anglo Saxons. The joke among the other teams was, however, that they hardly ever had any cases, and the jobs they did get were often unusual. They received intelligence that a particular batch of heroin that had the potential to cause lethal harm was on British

streets. When they investigated they found out it was contamin-
ated with uranium. It turned out that Russian and Ukrainian
criminals, in the years following the Chernobyl nuclear power
disaster, had planted poppies in the exclusion zone around
the stricken power plant. The drugs were so radioactive we had
to buy Geiger counters for the frontline staff trying to seize
the shipments.

They also investigated a consignment of pink heroin, which
was considered to be seven times stronger than regular opioids.
They traced this back to Iranian smugglers. After the revolu-
tion in 1978, when many Iranians fled the country, the only
way they could get their money out was to bring heroin and
the trade had continued. We helped the team out by providing financial details on some of their suspects, who nearly
always lived in affluent areas of London, like Knightsbridge or
Kensington and we were often at the Bank Melli on the High
Street there.

A more operational case we helped on was when the Golfs
were in Leicester, working on a joint operation with MI5, targeting a Sri Lankan smuggler who was also a terrorist. The
trafficker was a Tamil Tiger, and the intelligence services suspected he was sending the proceeds home to buy arms. No one
would have guessed he was helping facilitate an armed struggle
against a former British colony and strategic ally, because his
day job was as a milkman.

A few efforts had been made to get close to him to secure
the evidence needed to put him away, but nothing was working.
Rather than give up, or waste months trying to make contact,
MI5 apparently took matters into their own hands. One morning the milkman suffered a terrible accident. He was driving his
milk float downhill when it careered out of control and crashed.

He was taken to hospital and was out of action for some time afterwards.

It was only later that one of my colleagues, who had been on the ground in Leicester, told me what happened.

'They fixed his brakes,' he said. 'We were never going to put him away, so next best option – put him out of action.'

It was a staggering admission and, if true, was certainly an effective way to get a result.

Our next case also involved terrorists – except these ones operated much closer to home.

CHAPTER 13

Stopping the rot

Even hard-bitten Customs investigators had to admit they hadn't seen anything quite like it.

In the process of seizing a tonne of cannabis that had come into Hornsey, north London, and arresting the smugglers responsible, who were all apprehended unpacking the gear, their fingerprints all over the boxes, officers from Drugs K – the Kilos – seized a video.

We suspected the drugs were for the IRA, as the Irish organiser behind the seizure was said to be one of the republican terrorists' top men in London, and we therefore believed the video might provide all kinds of evidence or intelligence, perhaps relating to mainland activity, or show the faces of other associates we might be able to trace. It showed none of that, and we weren't quite prepared for what was on it.

There was the main man, the boss, the one calling the shots who had masterminded the whole operation. We imagined, back in Ireland, he was a feared republican. Yet, there in the video, it appeared there were some responsibilities he had to delegate to his second in command. In the X-rated home movie, the boss revealed himself to be impotent, and that he liked to film his wife having sex with his sidekick. Evidentially, it added little to the investigation, but it definitely provided some entertainment.

What wasn't funny, however, was how the case progressed. The evidence was overwhelming. Among the other items seized during the arrests was an electronic personal organiser. On it were entries for people with names like 'Big Jack' in Cardiff and 'Jonno' in Birmingham, with figures next to them, like '20-' or '15K'. Whether this referred to kilogrammes or pounds we weren't certain, but it was obvious these were entries for their distribution network and related to previous consignments or the money they had paid.

When I produced the financial statement for the drugs team, it revealed that the smugglers were worth nearly £6 million. The drugs seized were just the latest in a string of importations. This was a well-established criminal enterprise.

The trial was at Wood Green Crown Court, traditionally a good venue for us. It was a stonewall case, and the prosecutor set the evidence out clearly with the defence unable to offer an alternative explanation. The jury didn't spend long deliberating, so I thought I'd head over to the court to hear the verdict.

'Not guilty,' the foreman said, and repeated for all four defendants.

I couldn't believe what I was hearing. The other Customs officers there exchanged looks of disbelief. The prosecution team looked equally stunned. Every single one of them were acquitted on all charges – even though their fingerprints were on the boxes. It was like the jury had been nobbled.

People might not think it goes on in this country, but that case showed that it was definitely still possible. Perhaps the Kilos made a mistake taking it to Wood Green. The seizure taking place at Hornsey might have influenced their decision. It had always been a happy hunting ground for Customs, but we had the power to take it anywhere we wanted. If a container came in through Dover it made sense to take the trial to Kent. Most of the Dover drugs cases were heard at Maidstone Crown Court, where the jury would likely be full of 'hang 'em and flog 'em' Tory voters. They didn't want drug traffickers in their crown courts, so there was a high conviction rate.

Not long after that Wood Green trial shock, I was tasked to Arbroath, in Angus, in the north-east of Scotland, to help an operational team with the financial side of a case. Heroin had been seized on a boat coming into the town. The smugglers were arrested, but the team flew them down to London to charge them, so it showed geography was not an issue.

A high-profile case a year earlier, in 1989, illustrated the dangers of taking a trial close to the home of the accused. Ken Dodd was one of the UK's favourite entertainers when the Inland Revenue discovered tax evasion offences dating back to 1973, involving sums totalling nearly £1 million. When the case came to Liverpool magistrates' court, Dodd was facing 27 charges. The inspector leading the investigation, David Hartnett, said the evasion was 'much more serious' than originally thought.

On the night before the trial, Dodd had appeared on stage with Liverpool legends like Cilla Black and Jimmy Tarbuck, supporting families who had been affected by the Hillsborough tragedy just two months previously, when 97 people died. The following morning, he failed to appear for his trial, having been diagnosed with a cardiac arrhythmia. When the trial did finally get underway four days later, the courtroom was packed.

Brian Leveson QC, who later conducted the phone-hacking inquiry, laid out the case against him on charges of being a common-law cheat and false accounting. Tax investigators had found one account in Jersey and six accounts on the Isle of

Man into which Dodd had deposited £406,000, a sum that had grown to £777,453 with interest, which he had failed to mention either to his accountants or to the Inland Revenue.

Leveson described how Dodd liked to be paid two fees after an appearance – one settled with a cheque and put through the books, the other in cash and not declared.

Dodd, who was notorious throughout his career for being miserly, splashed out on the best defence money could buy in George Carman. The QC cast doubt on the professionalism of Dodd's former accountant Reginald Hunter, as well as on the advice given to the entertainer by the London-based account-ancy firm Grant Thornton, which had carried out an audit of his finances. Carman also expressed bafflement that the Inland Revenue had not interviewed Hunter as part of their investi-gation. This three-pronged attack would prove effective, even though the case revealed Dodd had kept £330,000 in cash in the attic of his home in Knotty Ash, a suburb of Liverpool. The comedian claimed he hoarded the cash because he thought the country was on the brink of civil war. He also said keeping large amounts of cash close made him feel like a star and gave him a 'feeling of security and accomplishment'.

The upshot was that, despite the strong case against Dodd, Customs didn't want to get involved. They saw the writing on the wall. To try him in Liverpool, amid the mood at the time, in a city still hurting from the deaths of football fans at the home of my team Sheffield Wednesday in an FA Cup semi-final, was always going to be a tall order. You were never going to get a Liverpool jury to convict and that's what happened. He was acquitted on all charges and walked free.

Customs had enjoyed more success with a similarly high-profile case two years previously, when the former champion jockey Lester Piggott was jailed for three years, after being found guilty of VAT and tax fraud, totalling £3.25 million.

Piggott, whose status as one of the greats was cemented after he rode nine Derby winners, had an estimated personal fortune of £20 million at the time Customs launched its joint investigation with Inland Revenue, amusingly codenamed Centaur, after the half-man, half-horse beast of Greek mythology. The investigators discovered the jockey had used different names to move his income into secret bank accounts in Switzerland, Singapore, the Cayman Islands and the Bahamas. They found he failed to declare £1,359,726 from additional riding income and, for fourteen years he omitted income of £1,031,697 from bloodstock operations. Piggott had come to an agreement with racehorse owners to take a percentage of stud money. Allegedly, every time they sold the sperm of a champion horse, he got a cut and didn't pay the tax and VAT on it.

The investigation became the biggest individual income tax-dodging case ever brought in Britain and the sentence was the highest to be passed for a personal tax fraud.

It showed the hubris of the man that he signed false declarations to the Inland Revenue during three successive inquiries into his tax affairs between 1970 and 1985. The judge even said that Piggott had misled his own accountants until the matter was 'forced out' of him.

For the officers on the case, it was a tremendous result. One of them shared some insight into Piggott's meanness. A trainer told him he had been at Deauville-La Touques Racecourse, in Normandy, with Piggott and both of their wives. It was a hot day and all four of them were in Piggott's Rolls Royce, when he spotted an ice cream van. He stopped, walked back to the vendor, got two ice creams and brought them back to the car.

The trainer said: 'Lester, there's four of us in the car, not just you and your wife.'

Piggott replied: 'No, these are both for me.'

He didn't even buy his wife one. Somebody that mean was going to take a fall sometime.

| | |

Customs officers routinely shared stories – and the good thing about the Whiskies was we regularly liaised with drugs teams on unusual cases.

One of our junior guys, Ben Reilly, was helping the Tangoes, who covered synthetic substances, like amphetamines, but also handled cocaine cases when required. One such case, for which Ben was doing the financial checks, resulted in the arrest of a Russian socialite who was a prominent cocaine supplier. One of her clients was King Hussein of Jordan and one of the more colourful details that came out during the investigation was that the now-deceased member of the royal family liked to put the white powder on the end of his penis. Ben's job was to interview the Russian in Holloway prison, where she was being kept on remand, awaiting trial. He wanted to give her an opportunity to explain how she came to have such considerable financial assets, for someone who appeared to never have a day job. Unless she came up with a credible explanation, we'd seize her assets. When Ben arrived for their meeting, he went into their private room to find her standing on the table, pleasuring herself and looking decidedly frantic. Clearly she wasn't adapting to prison life well.

As was normal for these sorts of interviews, the defendant refused our offer. It meant we could go to court and say we had asked for an explanation, but they declined to provide one.

Due to the power of assumption in the new law, we could allege – and courts could assume – that drug dealers had not earned their wealth legitimately. If a convicted drug trafficker had a £3-million house but there was no record of them ever earning a penny legally, we could assume they've been doing this for a while and therefore we were going to take everything off them. It was very draconian legislation, but effective. Unless they could say where the money came from, we would assume it was the proceeds of drug trafficking, and we'd ask the judge to apply these assumptions.

The civil service was then into Thatcher's business mania of applying private sector practices, like increased competition and performance-related pay, into the public sector, so investigators could earn big bonuses to top up their pay. The civil service bureaucrats set targets for us as assumed drugs money, not cash collected. We would often get assumptions of £1 million while the defendant had gambled or guzzled it all away, so the Confiscation Order, based on current net assets, was for two bob and the case eventually yielded tuppence.

Sometimes, though, we needed a helping hand to find the proceeds of crime. In my next case we were assisting the Victors, the cocaine and cannabis confiscation team, who had been helping the Romeos, carrying out a huge investigation into a notorious crime family from west London. They were like the Krays and their network extended throughout the south-west of England. For years, this family had been running riot and had seemed untouchable. They had been able to corrupt the police and, although Customs had long suspected they were behind several large cocaine importations, it had been hard to get the evidence needed to prosecute because they had a secret weapon at their disposal that, for us, was particularly galling.

They had what was known as a rip-off team (ROT) at Heathrow Airport. This was when a criminal organisation penetrated an airport or port by securing jobs there for fellow criminals, or corrupted workers already there, to help facilitate their importations. Whenever a large shipment came into Heathrow, their cohorts would take the drugs and bypass Customs control. Unfortunately, this problem was more widespread than we'd like to admit. It wasn't just confined to the one gang or at one airport, and the ROTs knew all the local duty men and women by sight and could usually smell an undercover operation a mile off, even with investigators from other areas of the country.

The investigation into this family was prolonged and extensive, but eventually Customs got word of a huge shipment – 153 kilos of cocaine and two tonnes of cannabis – coming into Southampton. Even with rip-off teams in place at Southampton, the traffickers weren't careful enough to avoid detection, and it was the largest haul of its kind ever made in Britain at the time.

The Romeos and Victors worked the case. Following on from the seizure, they had intelligence on several of the traffickers, thanks to some telephone intercepts by Alpha. We were in pursuit of the drug money, and I joined them on a search of a target's house on the day of the knock, because there was information that a large quantity of cash was on the premises.

We searched the house completely but couldn't find anything tangible. Alpha rang the senior officer and asked if we'd been successful.

'Negative,' the officer told them.

'You've missed the fucking money!' came the response.

He told them we'd searched everywhere.

'Have you searched the garden?'

'Yes.'

'Well, look under the paving stones.'

As a rule, we didn't usually start ripping gardens apart to find dirty cash, unless we had a tip off. Clearly, Alpha were party to some very specific intelligence.

We started lifting the slabs and, lo and behold, found packages buried there. When we opened them up they were full of bank notes. Once it was all counted it totalled over £100,000.

Now we had a strong case. When you can show a seizure of cocaine and cannabis and bags of cash that were stashed under paving stones, it can hugely influence the jury's mind. Our success was only part of the story, however. Alpha had intercepted calls between the gang's Spanish-speaking suppliers. They enlisted the help of a fantastic finance officer from DFIB, Sally Carter, who could speak Spanish, to translate what was being said. With her help, more cash was seized, and it turned into one of Customs' biggest ever cases. By the time it came to court, the total involved was £70 million. The head of the family was convicted of importing cocaine and cannabis at Winchester Crown Court and jailed for 25 years. There was no suspicion of jury nobbling this time.

Sally made a name for herself when she was rewarded with a jeroboam of champagne for being the first to recover a million pounds from an asset seizure. When the Spanish Gardia Civil's equivalent of Alpha supplied a tip-off on ex-pat criminals over there, she often flew out to help them, sometimes for a month at a time. Among the criminals they targeted was the Great Train Robber Charlie Wilson, who was lording it up in Marbella following his release from prison, having forged a new career as one of the biggest drug traffickers on the Costa del Crime. Back in 1987, during the joint Anglo-Soviet cannabis operation, the major drug smuggler Jimmy Rose had been caught by police and was in custody. Rose wanted to tell police the mastermind of the operation was another criminal, Roy 'The Lump' Adkins, who was then on the run from the law, in the hope he might get a lenient sentence. Rose's wife had rung Wilson – an associate of the two criminals – to ask his permission to name Adkins. Wilson explored the possibility with an associate of Adkins but two days later the Lump narrowly avoided capture when Dutch police raided his hideout just moments after he'd left. Adkins was furious, blamed Wilson for exposing his hideout, and branded the train robber a grass. On 23 April 1990, Wilson was at his villa preparing a barbecue when a young man turned up, supposedly with a message from Adkins' associate. After a brief exchange, the youth kicked Wilson in the groin, punched him in the face, breaking his nose and shot him twice, once in the neck.

Spanish Alpha were listening in live when, just minutes later, they heard Wilson's wife on the phone to an associate in London screaming: 'Charlie's been shot!'

It was interesting the number of old school gangland criminals who had entered the drugs trade. When I was on the Uniforms, Henry Black told me a lot of armed robbers had decided to make a career change in the light of a switch in police policy. After some high-profile and violent robberies, the police had adopted a shoot-to-kill strategy. They wouldn't wait until fired upon; they would just shoot any armed robbers on sight as they left the bank.

The gangs who had previously focused on robberies changed tactics, and they started to appear on our radar. Customs began investigating them for drug trafficking and VAT fraud, especially in the bullion trade and contrived insolvencies, where criminals would set up a new firm, like a plant hire business, issue £10-million worth of false invoices purporting to buy JCBs or cranes, submit their quarterly tax return showing a VAT payment of £2 million, but with no income yet, so generating an automatic rebate for this sum. In the old days, VAT offices sent out staff to confirm such refunds, for instance, checking if such JCBs were sitting in the yard, but that didn't fit the Tory ethos of trader control (allowing businesses to control themselves) to reduce bureaucrats (of whom, when a tax barrister, Thatcher had developed a distaste). Back in the tobacco factory in Sheffield, where I used to work, they eventually got rid of the roles of three Customs officers working there and let the company seal the containers themselves. This was all part of the Thatcher ethos.

The problems of rip-off teams continued to escalate at airports and ports. The issue wasn't helped by another of Thatcher's policies – privatising the docks. Overnight, much of the work done by staff was now being contracted out. At Liverpool, when this happened, one smuggling gang formed a company with some dockers who'd been just laid off, to win the contract to unload the containers. Other gangs sent people to apply for jobs on site, so they penetrated several key ports and airports, either individually or as groups.

We investigated another case where a group of criminals, who were known armed robbers and drug traffickers, formed a cleaning company that won the contract to clean branches of Barclays bank. What better way to scope out potential targets than by working in them beforehand?

Corruption, in all guises, was a seemingly never-ending problem – and even our own Customs teams were not immune to it.

CHAPTER 14

IIIIIIIIIIIIIIIIIIIIIIIIIIIIIIIIIIIIIIIIIIIIIIIII

Dirty tricks

It was the last race of the day, the King George V Handicap at Royal Ascot. The crowd's excitement, which had been building throughout the day, reached fever pitch as the second favourite, Ile de Chypre, pulled away in the final furlong.

With the line in sight, the bay horse, ridden by Greville Starkey, streaked ahead and looked certain to win by several lengths. Just yards from victory, however, Ile de Chypre suddenly veered off course and reared, unseating Starkey and gifting the race to his competitors.

The incident in 1988, though shocking, seemed to be one of those unfortunate things that happened now and then in racing, and not entirely out of character for a horse who had shown signs of a questionable temperament previously, even earlier on in that very race. But the events of that day were suddenly cast in a new light a year later, at Southwark Crown Court, during the trial of a car dealer accused of being part of a conspiracy to supply cocaine.

The prosecution claimed James Laming had links to a $15-million Peruvian drugs gang. Banknotes found in his car had traces of cocaine on them. He was also accused of possessing a quantity of the white powder worth £100,000. But Laming claimed the cash was money that had been paid out by on-course bookmakers after he'd won at the races. As far as explanations went for the presence of otherwise unexplained wealth, it was certainly novel, but that wasn't all. Laming claimed he'd pulled off an amazing coup at Ascot. It was he who had caused Ile de Chypre to fall – by using a stun gun disguised as a pair of binoculars.

The stun gun worked, the Peckham businessman's defence council said, by using a high-frequency sound that was inaudible to the human ear, but terrified animals. Jonathan Goldberg QC, told the court his client developed the device himself, using information taken from the *Encyclopaedia Britannica*. Mr Goldberg said the effect on a passing racehorse would be 'equivalent in human terms to a hideous, ear-piercing shriek'. The jury was then shown a video of Ile de Chypre's erratic behaviour just as he was about to secure victory.

Mr Goldberg said the conspiracy had nothing to do with drugs – but was to 'undermine the entire system of racecourse betting'.

He held up a large pair of binoculars, attached to a leather case, and told the court: 'It looks like an ordinary pair of black racing binoculars. But take off the lens caps and you see what looks like the backside of a jet engine.'

He said the lenses had been removed and replaced by two high-power transducers, which were basically a pair of loud-speakers of 'very high power indeed'.

The money would be won by 'laying off' a favourite or second-favourite in a race, which meant betting against the winning horse. Having such a device meant his client was in a unique position to ensure that the horse lost, Mr Goldberg said. The trial took an even stranger turn when Starkey provided three ponies for the stun gun to be tested upon, and two apparently behaved erratically.

Laming's defence caused the case to pause while the prosecution inspected the device. However, questions remained over how he could be sure to hit his target horse from more than 70 feet away. He was also unable to explain exactly how he managed to profit from the Ascot fall. Laming and his two co-defendants claimed they only used the gun once, on Ile de Chypre, and did not bet on that race. Laming said he was caught before he had a chance to use the gun again.

Despite the colourful defence, Laming was eventually convicted of being involved in the drug plot and of taking part in a conspiracy to supply cocaine. However, his sensational claims sent shock waves through the racing world. The Jockey Club took the allegations seriously and put Britain's racetracks on notice to look out for such ultrasonic 'stun guns' that might have been capable of affecting horse races from the stands. It vowed to prosecute anyone found with such a device at a track.

But the story of how such a device existed that could nobble horses and fix the outcome of a race also caused interest within the Customs Investigation Division.

A new senior officer had joined the Whiskies, Martin Sinclair. Initially he kept himself to himself, and I wanted to know more about our new addition, so asked one of his former associates what he was like. The officer told me how one of the clerks in their old department in Essex once showed him the local paper and directed his attention to the letters page. One regarded a recent planning application to the council to turn Sinclair's big, detached house into a nursing home. The correspondent fully supported the application.

'I couldn't work out why I was being shown the letter but, when it was pointed out who had written it, I was shocked to see my name! Sinclair had obviously faked a letter supporting his own planning application. That's what he's like.'

Sinclair was clearly a bit of an eccentric – and he had taken a keen interest in a case Alpha was working on. Interestingly, they had intelligence on a drug trafficking gang with links to the Mafia, who were importing heroin, but were also apparently trying to nobble horses. They too had a stun gun and the chatter over the telephone calls told how they were able to put someone at the finishing post to spook the runners and fix the races.

While they were trying to build the case against the criminals, Alpha and Sinclair paid close attention to the next race the gang hoped to influence. They became convinced they knew in advance what the winner would be in a certain race, at a time and place revealed from listening in to telephone calls. Sinclair went round the ID teams collecting as much tea money as he could to put on the race. He managed to scoop up nearly a grand. Some of the Alpha officers expected to be filling their boots too. It was all set. All they needed to do was wait and watch their bet come in. Whatever happened, they lost. Not only were Sinclair's hopes of making a killing gone, but so too was our tea money, which usually funded a massive Christmas piss-up.

It served the officers right for trying to cash in on privileged information, however dodgy. Sadly, that type of behaviour was not solely confined to speculative gambling. As was the way with many big organisations, once people had been there a long time, they became institutionalised, lost their ethics and were more susceptible to corruption.

An ID officer who used to be based on the frontline at Dover told me how easy it was for Customs colleagues to smuggle goods through ports.

'Just go through the red channel,' he said. 'If you do that you are making a declaration. If your mates at Dover or Heathrow choose not to tax you it means you get to go through duty-free. If you go through the green channel and don't declare anything you should be paying tax on then you're smuggling.'

Many do it, apparently.

A lot of unethical behaviour came back to the issue of staffing. The government was always looking to cut back on numbers and that was detrimental to morale among staff who felt overworked and undervalued, so they looked for other ways to find perks.

Another Customs officer, who worked at Hull port, told me of the time a government minister paid them a visit. He asked them when they last had a drug bust. When the officers told him it was five years ago, he asked what the point was of keeping a Customs presence there. One of the senior officers countered by asking when any of the UK's major airports last suffered a bomb attack. It had never happened. Would that be a reason to get rid of the security staff? It was quite a strong argument to make to your departmental minister, and the politician could only nod in agreement. It's astonishing the case had to be made in the first place.

Unfortunately, that was the attitude further up the tree. They only thought in terms of numbers, not people. Another officer at Dover told me how he'd once stopped someone coming into the port. He didn't have the benefit of any intelligence. He just made the decision on the spot.

The suspect even asked him: 'Why are you stopping me?'

The officer said: 'I recognised your face because I arrested you six years ago. You were bringing in drugs then, were a repeat offender and were still making regular trips in and out of this port.'

He detained him, searched him and found he was smuggling gear in again.

If you just slash numbers to save money you lose that experience.

We even had our tame judge at Southwark asking us to sort out Heathrow colleagues who had taxed and fined him for not declaring the Rolex he'd just bought in New York. He wanted a refund. Nice.

Attempts by the government to improve morale were counterproductive. Under Thatcher, the Conservatives brought in a bonus scheme, to inspire a more competitive, energised workforce. They introduced a marking system where we were awarded points for our successes. It sounded reasonable in theory, but in practice it was flawed. For a start, the system was uneven. Commercial fraud was considered more valuable than drugs work, so you got more points for catching someone illegally importing rice than a kilo of heroin. Plus, some of the operational teams could spend two years on a single drug case and, for any number of reasons, it didn't come off. They wouldn't get a bonus. It created the wrong sort of culture, but that was a hallmark of Thatcher's government.

|||

Martin Sinclair might have missed out on his Mafia race-fixing tip, but that didn't put him off trying to cash-in on other scams. The late eighties were a time of mass privatisations and in 1990 it was the turn of the electricity companies. He wanted me to join him on a trip to Royal Leamington Spa to take a witness statement from a building society worker for a potential money laundering case. On the way up, however, he made several stops to open accounts at different building societies in a range of different names. The privatisation shares were capped at 1,000 shares and limited to one application per person. By opening new accounts in the name of all sorts of people, from second cousins to Uncle Tom Cobley, he hoped to make multiple applications for shares he could then sell on the day of flotation. Essentially, here was a senior Customs officer laundering money.

That wasn't the only aspect of Sinclair's personality I found objectionable. Once we got the witness statement we needed, he suggested we drive on twelve miles to Stratford-Upon-Avon to watch a Shakespeare play on a wet Wednesday, instead of returning home to mid-week footy on the telly. We had just taken our seats when he warned me he suffered from 'hereditary flatulence'. He was the only known case, apparently. As if on cue, he emitted a loud raspberry and a horrible scent filled the air. By the interval he had dispersed half the audience, made up mostly of American tourists. None of them came back to their seats for the second half.

With this sort of behaviour, it was no surprise we didn't get on. He embodied the lapse in ethics and low-level corruption that seemed to invade every level of the service. Even some major investigations were at the mercy of questionable moral judgements.

An example of this was a massive cocaine bust in which our team was asked to help the Romeos. The investigation had been several months in the making. The Romeos had been tracking the Liverpool-born criminal Curtis Warren's organisation, who they had intelligence was shipping in cocaine from Colombia's Cali Cartel. Warren, the son of a Norwegian merchant seaman and shipyard worker, had been employed as a nightclub bouncer in the city. It was while working on the doors that he got to know the local drug dealers, by letting them into the club and befriending them and learning how they operated.

It wasn't long before he teamed up with another drugs trafficker, Brian Charrington, a big player in the North East. Charrington had vast riches and, ideally for their purposes, a yacht. The two of them travelled to France on British visitor passports – simple documents, valid for one year, which enabled travel to European countries. Once there, they used their standard, ten-year passports to fly to Venezuela, which the Colombian cartels had flooded with cocaine. The pair came up with the plan to import huge amounts of coke from Venezuela, in steel boxes sealed inside lead ingots, which were impossible to x-ray and hard to cut open. Customs were on to them in 1991, and stopped the boat and found the ingots, but when they drilled into one they found nothing. Having no option but to let them proceed, it was only when Dutch police later advised them, following a tip-off, that the drugs were in steel containers inside the ingots that they realised their mistake. A second shipment of 907 kilograms of cocaine, however, was already on its way to the UK.

At the time of the knock there must have been around 300 Customs officers in the Liverpool area, ready to take down various members of Warren's criminal enterprise. The Whiskies were there to arrest the money launderers. I was with Jack Burns, and our target had been buying houses on Merseyside, passing suitcases filled with £100,000 at a time to a bent solicitor who facilitated the purchases.

We expected to come face to face with a hardened criminal, with years of experience. Instead, our money man was just a kid. He had recently turned twenty but looked about fifteen. He'd been going around the Wirral buying up houses. When we interviewed him at a Liverpool police station he had no credible explanation for the cash. He muttered that a 'friend' had transferred it into his account but couldn't say who the friend was or give details of the account.

Our team's involvement was limited to the questioning of suspects like this, but as the case progressed, it exposed deep issues within UK law enforcement. The seizure was one of the biggest ever made in the UK and 28 people were arrested, but the prosecution was scuppered when police revealed Warren's associate Charrington was an informant for two officers from the North-East Regional Crime Squad. Customs pressed ahead with the prosecution and in Newcastle Crown Court it was claimed that Warren was so well informed he made the lead ingots extra thick because he knew precisely the length of Customs' largest drill bit. Eventually, though, north-east Tory MP Tim Devlin intervened on the police's behalf and Customs were forced to drop the charges against Charrington. The case against Warren collapsed and he was acquitted, along with all his gang members.

The outcome was a sore one for Customs. Not only did Warren gloat to officers, on his release, that he was 'off to spend my £87 million from the first shipment and you can't touch me', but months later Customs officers spotted one of Charrington's police handlers driving a £70,000 BMW that had previously belonged to the informant.

With Warren free to continue to grow his empire, some Customs officers suspected he might have amassed as much as £150 million. Certainly, after that let off from the police, he became the richest criminal in British history, and he once appeared on the *Sunday Times* Rich List.

When we were working on the case he was based in the Netherlands and he became Interpol's Target One. Vast sums of his cash were believed to have been stashed in tax havens and Swiss banks, some of it in luxury property in Liverpool's upmarket Wapping Dock development, which, gallingly, was situated opposite the Customs museum.

In all, Customs believed he had bought around 200 properties in the north-west of England, as well as office blocks. He also had mansions in Liverpool, the Netherlands and Spain, where he also owned a casino.

Although he splashed the cash, Warren wasn't like your usual British crook. He didn't drink, smoke or use the drugs he imported. He was said to have possessed a photographic memory for telephone numbers and numbers of bank accounts. He didn't have anything written down. There were no notebooks, computers or records of any kind. It was all stored in his head. He never called contacts by their names but stuck to code words. His ability to evade justice granted him an unlimited credit line from the Colombian cocaine cartels and cannabis traffickers across Eastern Europe.

When Dutch police finally arrested Warren in 1996, they raided his villa and found an arsenal of weapons, hand grenades, crates with hundreds of CS gas canisters, 400 kilos of cocaine, 1,500 kilos of cannabis resin, 60 kilos of heroin, 50 kilos of ecstasy, plus hundreds of thousands in cash. The whole haul was estimated to be worth £125 million. Warren was sentenced to twelve years in jail. When it came to recovering his assets, however, only £20 million of that estimated £150 million fortune could be found, and none of that could be legally touched or confiscated by Dutch police, British police or Interpol, because they had to prove it was acquired illegally through drugs.

Around the time of the Curtis Warren investigation, we visited the Netherlands to see their equivalent of Alpha. I was staggered by what I saw. They had a far more relaxed attitude to drug crime, but they took commercial fraud much more seriously than we did. They could arrange telephone intercepts for tax fraud cases, which we didn't do. I felt we should adopt this policy.

It was also interesting to learn that whenever they'd bugged someone's phone, whether it led to an arrest or not, they had to tell the target their calls had been intercepted. In the UK our regime was very hush-hush, and authorisation for any Alpha inquiries had to be signed by the Home Secretary personally.

Like many other countries, the Dutch could use intercepts for evidence, whereas in the UK it was only used for intelligence. This was frustrating as it could have been an even more invaluable tool. It would have enabled us to find out who was behind what were obvious front companies for money laundering. Often, when we looked for details of directors or traced the names given they had as much credit history as tramps on the street. With intercepts we could have got straight to the heart of who was behind them.

We also had the added issue at that time of Alpha not understanding money laundering work. They would only approve an intercept for a 'serious crime' – sentences that carried prison terms over two years, up to fourteen years. Customs offences had several real jail term limits for fraud offences – one was two years and above that was seven or fourteen years. There was therefore justification for telephone intercepts, Alpha just chose to ignore that fact.

Meeting with the Dutch investigators highlighted the difference in attitudes. The Dutch had a very pro-business culture. That laissez-faire approach enabled Rotterdam to become the

biggest port in the world, especially when it came to importing oil. With its deep-water tank terminals, Rotterdam had
more oil than Saudi Arabia. That said, however, the Dutch did
clamp down on illegal practices. Legitimate businesses were
allowed to flourish but they hammered corruption. If they
extended that approach to drug traffickers, big players like
Warren wouldn't have based themselves there. They knew the
Netherlands was a soft touch on narcotics.

|||

After two years with the Whiskies, I was starting to feel frustrated, seeing more evidence of our limitations, rather than what
we could achieve. I was sensing a lack of progress. It appeared
to me that, in the Civil Service, the policy makers were the
ones who got the plaudits, not the operational people, like in
business. The hierarchy didn't seem to care about the people on
the ground, only how they could further their careers. It felt
to me that, in the private sector, the opposite was true – it was
the rank and file who did the work, that got the praise and the
promotions, not the pen pushers.

It didn't help that the senior officer I had huge respect for,
Jack Burns, was promoted to run his own VAT fraud team. He
was one of the experienced people who did try to push people
on. In the two years I had worked with him, I was marked
'fitted' for promotion twice on my annual appraisal, but since
Sinclair arrived, my chances of moving up were as remote as
ever. We had a mutual distrust of each other, and he knew I'd
been put there to try to reign him in.

I felt it was time for a new challenge.

My personal situation had improved considerably during
this period, however. About a year on from that first phone call

from the EIA, Charmian Gooch and I became a couple. Our relationship had developed quite rapidly and before long we moved in together.

By this time, I had bought a flat in Queen's Park, which, although not as salubrious as Maida Vale, where I used to live, was still in Westminster borough. Unintentionally, I benefitted indirectly from the homes for votes scandal, where the Conservative leader of Westminster Council, Shirley Porter, was accused of gerrymandering, after moving homeless people into condemned accommodation and authorising the selling-off of council houses to people more likely to vote Tory. She was later found guilty of wilful misconduct and ordered to repay £36 million. Although I didn't buy from the council, the flat I purchased was one of those sold off under her regime. It was a pretty rough area back then, but the council tax was only £36 a year and it was in zone two for the underground.

When Charmian and I got together we moved into a flat in Hampstead, where from our front room, she set up an NGO called Global Witness, with a couple of her colleagues from EIA. The organisation focused on natural resource-related conflict and corruption, as well as environmental and human rights abuses, and it went from strength to strength. Years later its report into the international diamond trade, which was funding the Angolan Civil War, formed the basis of the movie *Blood Diamond*, starring Leonardo DiCaprio. In recognition of its campaigns, Global Witness was nominated for a Nobel Peace Prize.

As my frustrations grew, it was time to find a new role. I was still a junior investigator, albeit with considerable experience under my belt, and my time on the Whiskies was coming to an end. Customs didn't want you spending more than three years on any branch or team, to deter corruption. In some instances, target teams virtually lived with their suspects for years.

When it was time to move, I could name a preference for the type of team I wanted to join. I thought working on an operational drugs unit could be the challenge I craved. Moving away from the money launderers, it would be chance to work on the frontline, tackling the drug smugglers right at their point of entry to our shores.

Only one question at my interview gave me the slightest concern: 'How are you on a boat?'

CHAPTER 15

|||||||||||||||||||||||||||||||||||||||||||||||||||

Operation Sea Chase

Clearly, I didn't have my father's sea legs. As someone who felt queasy on the Dover to Calais ferry, perhaps joining Drugs J (the Juliets) – or the boat team as they were commonly called – wasn't the best move.

Here we were, speeding our way west along the English Channel. It was my first time on board a Customs cutter vessel, with a crew of hardened sailors, and I was trying my best to stop throwing up over the side.

I had joined the cutter at Portsmouth. It was one of five we had patrolling UK waters. It was an impressive boat, one of the Protector class vessels. It was 42-metres long, with a top speed of 26 knots. It carried a seven-metre rigid inflatable boat (RIB), in case we needed to board another craft, and a four-metre rescue boat. Thankfully, I wasn't required to go on the RIB as, even aboard the cutter, every roll of the sea churned my stomach. The boat team had crews operating on a fortnight-on, fortnight-off rota. I wasn't assigned to those crews but, like them, I had a pager and was now on call 24 hours a day. You never knew when you would get the shout to join an operation. The boats could carry out stop-and-search routines on suspicious vessels within twelve miles of land and, like the other operational teams, acted on intelligence from Alpha or informants.

Drugs J was one of the cannabis teams. This job was a joint operation involving Bristol ID and Irish Customs. We were waiting for a RIB to make its way to Ireland from Morocco, with a tonne of cannabis on board and were on standby in case it turned east and tried to land its shipment in Devon. From Portsmouth, we headed along the south coast towards Plymouth.

The smugglers were an ingenious outfit. We'd had intelligence they'd done a successful run before, coming into Devon and then transferring the entire shipment to several horse boxes, before driving to a warehouse in Exeter. It was perfect cover for moving around the country lanes – who would think to stop a horse box in Devon? It was a ruse most of the team had never seen before and highlighted the enterprise of these gangs. They took all the gear to London, to another warehouse, where we suspected the cannabis was cut and distributed.

We had this current operation meticulously planned, but we were in the dark as to exactly where in Devon this importation would arrive. While we patrolled the Devon coast – one of two boats that covered the Channel – another drugs team was ready on land in Ireland. We also had the Special Boat Service (SBS), the Royal Navy's elite special forces, on standby.

After several hours at sea, we finally got word. The RIB had been spotted, maintaining its course to Ireland. Customs teams there would intercept it. We were stood down. That was the way of the boat team. You could watch for something to happen four times and only once would it lead to a seizure.

Although the operation didn't provide a dramatic conclusion for our team, it was impressive to see the resources at our disposal. Drugs J had a sailor, with his own boat, who assisted with undercover operations. When cooperating informants had smugglers wanting to bring in an importation, they were given his details. It was good way to penetrate organisations. Whenever he was tasked, we would go out in a cutter to follow him discreetly, often as far as 50 miles away, for security. Sometimes this could mean tailing him from Morocco to Southampton. We needed to keep a watchful eye on him because there was every chance, due to bad weather, that he might have to put into a different port than originally planned.

He was an example of a specialist operator working undercover, but it was a source of frustration how limited our options usually were when it came to undercover operations. For instance, during my time at Customs, we didn't have one female undercover officer, nor did we have anyone from an ethnic minority. So many cases involving Asian smugglers fell down because we lacked a credible infiltrator.

Given the nature of the operations, the Juliets were one of the teams who could be called upon to make an interception at sea and seize drugs before a vessel made port. Such operations were fraught with difficulties – and danger. Often the officers were deciphering intelligence from a variety of sources, like the undercover officer driving the boat, an informant on board, drug liaison officers who were posted abroad in countries where the drugs were shipped from, or through Alpha's phone bugging. Sometimes they would also have to liaise with the intelligence services through GCHQ, or the pilot of a plane, which Customs also had at their disposal. On land, if rural surveillance was required, they could call on a special team called CROPS (Covert Rural Operations), Customs officers trained by the SAS who would literally embed themselves in the gardens of properties of suspected smugglers. They would dig holes in the ground, build makeshift observation points or hide in the gardens of suspects or of derelict buildings for days, sometimes weeks, on end. They were especially valuable if the targets were operating from remote premises not easily accessed by road.

Invariably, when information came in, Drugs J officers had to act quickly and decisively, especially if the intelligence suspected the smugglers were armed. As our cutters were not armed, the SBS provided our military back-up should things get serious. It was a similar story to operational teams on land. If there was a risk of violence, they had armed police as back-up.

Involving special forces was not done lightly and, usually, as much advance warning was given as possible. This was not always an option, however. We might have been able to forecast that a boat was coming in at a certain time, but it might only be as accurate as 'Bristol on Wednesday'. Sometimes this information came very late. Such operations were a moving feast. Details changed all the time.

In one operation, I learned the painful lesson the hard way, that it was always advisable to check where the SBS were before enlisting their help. We had a boat coming in near Southampton. The word was that they were a heavy gang, and armed. I asked my junior colleague to ring the Ministry of Defence and tell them we needed the SBS. He put in the request for Thursday morning at 6am in the Solent.

'No problem, we'll get them there,' the MoD said.

What I hadn't appreciated fully at the time was that the government, not long before Thatcher's resignation in 1990, introduced a new policy allowing each department to charge each other for services provided. It was designed to make them operate more like regular businesses and to help quantify inter-agency work (like drug smuggling, which Customs, a Treasury organisation, worked on the Home Office's behalf).

If we asked the police to help with some fingerprint analysis, they might send us a bill. If the police asked Customs to stop someone at Heathrow, we could have sent them a bill. If we asked the Laboratory of the Government Chemist to analyse some drugs or examine some questioned documents, they would bill us as they were on the list for privatisation. Of course, no one ever saw a cost/benefit for all this, or knew the expense involved in this extra pen and paper pushing.

I didn't instruct my junior colleague Jack Lloyd to ask any questions. Job done, we both thought, when he got the positive response. The SBS duly turned up as planned, but as it transpired they weren't needed. The operation passed off peacefully.

A month later the department received a bill from the MoD for £2 million.

When we investigated it turned out the SBS had been on a vessel in the middle of a training operation near Gibraltar. When they got our call, the MoD diverted a warship from the Mediterranean to Portsmouth.

Maybe if we'd known there was a huge cost involved we might have made a different call with the operation – or perhaps we would've paid it regardless. With drug smugglers, you can't pick and choose when you want to intercept them. Sometimes you only get one shot.

|||

A big problem we were finding in the early nineties were traffickers using high-speed RIBs to bring vast quantities of drugs ashore. These vessels had up to eight 250-horsepower outboard engines and could travel at speeds up to 60 knots, the equivalent of 70 miles per hour. RIBs were virtually undetectable to radar and were painted grey or black to make them less visible in the water. One of the senior officers told me smugglers from mainland Europe would fly across the Channel heading for the lights they could see from Dungeness nuclear power station, on the headland of southern Kent, from France and Belgium. He also said these super-powered vessels could get from Morocco to Ireland in four hours. There was no way our cutters would keep pace with them.

The Republic of Ireland was a favoured destination because traffickers considered it, along with the Netherlands, to be the soft belly of Europe and another gateway into the UK. To combat this Drugs J conducted a joint operation with their Irish counterparts, but it was an eye-opener to the contrast in powers. Irish Customs didn't have the power of arrest, like we did, and when the solitary police officer arrived to greet us it emerged he was also a part-time publican. That illustrated the stark contrast in resources. That operation wasn't a resounding success, but it did establish a route from Ireland to Liverpool, so from an intelligence perspective, it wasn't a wasted exercise.

My move to Drugs J, in 1991, coincided with some major changes to the ID. We had a new CIO, who, for the first time, did not have an investigations background. It was said the government had been worried about the ID getting out of control and so brought in high-flyer Doug Tweddle to try and restore some order. He was a nice guy, although perhaps a bit naïve, but once he was in the job he went native and completely embraced the investigations ethos and the hype, kudos and publicity around drug and fraud investigations, some of which included MPs who topped up their salaries with highly paid speeches, articles and appearances they failed to register for VAT – another example of Customs' wide-ranging power.

He was replaced a couple of years later by another former ID investigator, Dick Kellaway.

It's important to remember the political and diplomatic climate of the time. It was looking certain that Britain would sign the Maastricht Treaty in 1992, which would pave the way to create a European Union, signalling free movement of people and a removal of economic borders between member states. The Soviet Union had fallen apart, the Cold War was over and, basically, the intelligence services had nothing to do. They were effectively finished and were scraping around looking for work.

Within Customs, senior figures were starting to get paranoid. One of the first things the new CIO did was move the entire ID to Custom House. The New Fetter Lane office was vacated and every team joined DFIB by the river. Even Alpha was moved from the office in Victoria it shared with its police equivalent and the intelligence services, to the top floor of Custom House. It became an almost mythical, secret level, to which only certain officers had access and required two swipe cards, a code number and a thumbprint to enter. Casual visits were strictly forbidden and there was certainly no gossiping about cases in the corridor. The spooks had long wanted to do Customs work and so now we suddenly started seeing intelligence officers from MI5 and MI6 in Custom House.

Incidentally, the New Fetter Lane office had been next door to the *Daily Mirror* on Fleet Street. You used to hear Robert Maxwell's helicopter going by overhead. After he died mysteriously, off his yacht, in 1997, Steve Berry told me in no uncertain terms that it was no accident. Before his death it had been claimed he was a Mossad agent – and he was certainly given a lavish send off in Israel. Steve's theory was that he was murdered, most likely by the Palestinians.

Operationally, the changes didn't make that much of a difference for the boat team. We continued to receive jobs in the same way. We were a referred team, so although we helped other units, our jobs should've primarily come from airports and docks, as was the case with one investigation from Heathrow. The Customs officers at the airport had phenomenal experience and sophisticated computer programmes for targeting passengers and freight traffic. If something was not right with a consignment or the manifest, or there was something suspicious about its country of origin or destination, the computer would flag it to be checked.

When a consignment of cheap household furniture arrived all the way from Johannesburg, the computer highlighted a potential issue. When the items were searched they found half a tonne of cannabis stashed inside. The consignment seized was due to be going to a storage facility near the A40, run by Kuehne + Nagel, large international transporters of commercial freight. We went there waiting for the lorry to turn up to see who claimed the goods. Despite the computer's suspicions, there was no intelligence on who might be ready to claim it.

Eventually somebody did. It was a South African man, who was arrested, and we then connected him to a flat in Fulham, rented by a new suspect from Johannesburg. We went to raid this apartment, which was on the ground floor of a mansion block.

Everything was set up for a classic *Sweeney*-style raid, with everyone at the front door, except me. I went round the back to check if there was access to the communal gardens. As usual on knocks, some colleagues lost their head and common sense collapsed as they followed the herd.

When I saw the height of the gate into the garden, and the fact it was locked, I did wonder if anyone else on the team – many of whom were heavy drinkers with bellies to match – would be able to scale it.

I climbed the gate, trying not to rip my leather bomber jacket, and suddenly I saw someone running across the garden from the ground floor flat. There was nobody else with me. I was on my own.

The suspect looked like a bulked-up version of the celebrity chef Gordon Ramsay – broad, with a mess of blond hair and flushed face. He was halfway across the garden, heading for the neighbour's wall.

'Hey!' I called. 'He's here.'

My heart was pumping but I hoped he'd think there was a squad behind me. I didn't fancy trying to apprehend him over the ten-foot garden wall. He was a big guy. The shout did the trick. He stopped in his tracks. I ran over to him, rugby tackled him and wrestled him to the ground. A couple of my colleagues had managed, by then, to climb over the gate from the front of the building and they now joined me. I arrested and cautioned him and took him back inside the flat, where I started making contemporaneous notes in my pocketbook that was always on me.

In terms of evidence, we had nothing against this guy, but the fact I caught him fleeing from his house would look very suspicious in the eyes of a jury. It fell under *actus reus*, a guilty act.

'Of course, you'll be wondering who the informant is on this,' I said to him, while we were in the back of the car on the way to interview him.

There was no informant, but I wanted to sow disinformation

and chaos and put him and any colleagues on the back foot. He wasn't to know it had been a computer-generated interception at Heathrow. He just looked at me menacingly and, as he did throughout a two-day interrogation, remained silent. I wrote in my witness statement that I caught the suspect escaping.

We had been working with the Customs DLO in the South African Embassy here on the case and, a few days after his interview, their liaison at the consulate told me there had been a lot of activity over in Johannesburg. People linked to our suspects' organisation were going around desperately trying to establish who the informant was. And there was me just making it up to put him and his mate on the back foot before his interview. I hoped, if he had in his mind that we had an informant, it might destabilise him and prompt him to cooperate. How he managed to get the message out to his associates I'll never know.

When the case came to trial, we were no further forward against the second suspect. The guy who'd turned up at Kuhn + Nagel was bang to rights but had kept silent. This was obviously a very heavy organisation.

The second man's defence team attacked the flimsiness of our case, but when it was my turn to give evidence, I was able to show my contemporaneous notes that indicated he had tried to escape, so at least there was consistency.

As it turned out, the circumstances of the arrest, together with the seizure of the cannabis and the fact we were able to trace him from the goods the drugs were stashed in were enough to convince the jury, for they found him and his co-accused guilty and both got eight years in jail.

It wasn't the end of the story, however. He appealed against his conviction and was awarded a retrial. I gave evidence again but this time the jury weren't as easily convinced, and he walked free.

It was a disappointing outcome, but if I wanted to join an operational team for greater excitement then it looked like I had found it. It wouldn't be long before I was face to face with another suspect. And, once again, I was on my own.

CHAPTER 16

Anything to declare?

We were about to go in. Alpha were calling the shots, so we had to be ready. Any moment, we'd get the word – and the usual chaos would ensue.

We were out of sight, across from a warehouse, near Yiewsley, in Middlesex, awaiting the arrival of a large lorry carrying a tonne of cannabis that had come into north-west London. It was a joint operation between our fellow cannabis target team, Drugs B/C, and they had enlisted the help of as many other officers from the dope branch they could get. I was in a car with agent Carrie Daniels, who I'd first met on the Whiskies – the team her dad Kenny would later take over. She had now joined Branch 1 and Drugs B and C.

This was grade 'A', as we were apparently dealing with a top organisation of heavy London criminals that, as usual, had evaded the police forever and Customs for several years.

In between the industrial estate, where the warehouse was situated, and the spot where we were waiting, ran the Grand Union Canal, linking London with Birmingham. At the briefing, we'd only been given the layout of the front of the industrial park, which was where everyone was supposed to target once we got the nod. It just occurred to me, though, that if someone fled through the back and jumped in the canal, nobody would be on this side of the canal to stop them. As soon as we got 'the knock', the adrenalin would send everyone to the front.

Just then we heard a rumbling noise. It was the lorry. The order was to let it unload and then we would pounce, just when they were opening the boxes, leaving fingerprints all over them.

That moment when you know you're about to strike – but are just waiting for the word – always seems to last forever.

'Knock! Knock! Knock!'

There it was. That was our signal. As I predicted, everybody drove over the bridge and jumped out their vehicles and ran towards the entrance. I remained stationary in our vehicle, on the opposite side of the bridge to the warehouse, ignoring Carrie's shout to follow everyone else.

Moments later a man ran from the warehouse and, without hesitating, jumped straight into the canal. He swam towards our side and the bridge. I got out and walked down the towpath as he swam towards me, while Carrie stayed in the car and updated all on the radio about what was happening. I stood waiting for him to clamber out. Even though it was a hot summer's evening, he looked shocked and was shaking badly as he struggled to get out and onto the path. Remembering my BITs training, I grabbed him, helped him out, then forced him to stay on the ground but, as an added precaution, put my knee into his back as I cuffed him.

By now Carrie had joined me, shrieking: 'Mark, you're too aggressive.'

'Look at this,' I said.

He had a hefty sheath knife about a foot long. It was only when I grabbed him that I saw the flash of silver in the waistband of his jeans. Maybe he had been using it to break open the boxes when all hell broke loose, but I wasn't taking any chances.

It was practically a machete. If he had put that in me, I would have been dead in seconds.

Fortunately, he was so shocked he put up no resistance. Being a Drugs B/C officer, Carrie arrested and cautioned the suspect, who was taken off for treatment and then interviewed by her and another colleague.

The raid was a huge success. Dozens of arrests were made, and the cannabis seized. It should have been pats on the back all round while the drugs teams began preparing the paper-work needed for trial. My own statement took in not just 'the knock', but a connected job beforehand. Following Alpha's live intelligence, we had all been tasked to drive by a pub car park a few miles away to try to observe a meeting of a notorious East End criminal, who was organising the importation, and another gang member, who had been minding the consignment from Dover. However, as we glided past the pub, we only saw the minder, and so I noted in my pocketbook accordingly.

A few days later, a B/C case officer came up to me.

'This is your witness statement, sign it,' he said, thrusting a single piece of paper in front of me.

I looked over it. 'I'm not signing that,' I said.

The statement said I witnessed the two crooks meeting in the car park. Not only was it not true but it contradicted what was in my notebook.

'Why not?' he said.

'Because I didn't see any meeting happen,' I said.

I only saw one of the intended targets in the car park. If there had been a meeting arranged, either the other suspect didn't show up, and Alpha were clearly insisting he had, or I had missed it. But, obviously, so had everyone else, as we had all been instructed to drive by the pub car park.

'Alpha want this,' he said.

'I don't give a fuck what they want,' I said.

I wasn't prepared to lie and fit someone up. Whether or not their main target had been there I didn't know, but no one had witnessed it. I wondered what Carrie and the rest of the B/Cs had in their statements and notebooks.

In all my time as a Customs officer this was the only instance I was asked this – to fabricate evidence. It wasn't just about changing my statement. If I was called to give evidence at court, I would be asked to show my contemporaneous notes, copies of which would already have gone to the defence as unused material. And the notebooks were numbered and signed out by the team leader when issued. In them, I'd made a physical description of the one person I briefly saw and the registration number of a nearby BMW. How would I explain that?

From their phone intercepts, Alpha were convinced the meeting had taken place. They just couldn't prove it and their intelligence couldn't be used as evidence.

Was it because I was relatively new to the cannabis branch, that I was a guest on the investigations for Drugs B and C? I don't know. But I told him where to go. Just what sort of a cowboy outfit was this so-called top team?

I knew I had done the right thing, but that didn't stop me fearing I was going to be in trouble. Would my resistance be fed back to Alpha and give me a black mark against my name? It also made me wonder how often the doctoring of statements and notebooks went on. If that was commonplace, what other laws were broken?

When I first started in Uniforms, officers told stories of the times when a colleague on Drugs L, the Limas, used to beat up Turkish suspects in the cells and around Green Lanes in Harringay, so I'm sure that used to happen, but not during my time. In terms of fiddling evidence, however, there was always a great source of pride within Customs that we weren't like the police. At that time the cops were being dogged by the Birmingham Six and Guildford Four scandals. Customs didn't have anything like that against our reputation. Maybe times were a-changing.

There were the odd dodgy officers, like the SO Martin Sinclair on the Whiskies. However, because it was such a big, international institution, only around 20 per cent of officers were from London, with the rest from elsewhere in the UK. I think that played a part, because policing is very parochial. A detective in the East End is invariably investigating people he grew up with, so there can be an issue of skewed loyalties. That didn't happen in Customs, as its structure was national and much more complex. There were very few convictions of corruption, just a couple at Heathrow or the odd clerical officer who'd checked CEDRIC and the Police National Computer for some daft boyfriend with a grudge. More were dealt with and just disciplined internally to keep it quiet. But in the police corruption was endemic. In Stoke Newington, there was a case of police officers selling the coke they had seized in north London. I was told stories of the old days, of the infamous West Midlands Serious Crime Squad tying Irish bomber suspects to a disused railway line, telling them to confess or the nine o'clock to New Street would dismember them. We didn't have any of that. Not everyone was whiter than white, but, as far as I knew, no one took drugs or money from criminals. When we followed the money man on DFIB, and he left the bag full of cash in the taxi, it was there for the taking, but it never crossed our minds. It wasn't part of the culture. Officers might have smuggled their own goods in without paying tax, but they probably viewed that as a perk of the job; maybe the ID was starting to lose its discipline.

This was an attitude I encountered when we were sent to the Isle of Wight, in the winter of 1992, to gather intelligence on an organisation we had been told had set up near Shanklin. Our job was to carry out surveillance on target properties and we were to be there to help kit out a boat if it was needed for an undercover drug run. Fifteen of us descended on the island and, to keep knowledge of our presence there to a minimum, we avoided booking a hotel. Instead, we rented a cottage, in the middle of nowhere. It was absolutely freezing. The only thing that made it bearable was we were able to take advantage of the travel expenses. We were given an allowance of £67 a night, and the cottage cost each of us about £2 a night, allowing us to pocket a decent amount.

That wasn't enough for our senior officer (SO). Jim McDonald was a dour Scot, who lived up to the stereotype. He thought we should each save as much as we could and so insisted we only bought the cheapest supermarket food, which we cooked ourselves. When he went back to London and another SO, Dave Archer, took over, he had the opposite attitude. He wanted the best salmon and the finest wine, so that ate into our allowance, but made the month less miserable.

It was a very strange experience, being holed up in the countryside. All we had to go on was some sketchy intelligence from a new informant. Without Alpha or the cooperation of a participating informant, target work was extremely challenging. You always had to consider whether a new snout was genuine, or if they were just testing us, or checking out the resources we had at our disposal and our modus operandi. Perhaps they were even smuggling themselves and using us as the perfect cover, or they were creating a diversion and the real action was happening elsewhere. There had also been instances of informants stealing drugs off smugglers once they'd successfully been imported into the UK. It was just one of the risks when controlled deliveries were allowed to run live.

You simply didn't know what you were going to get with an informant. On another case, one of the bosses put me in touch with a son of his friend. He was a pilot, in his twenties, and claimed he been approached to bring drugs into the country. He was willing to be a participating informant. It sounded promising, but when I went to Eye airfield, an abandoned old RAF station for large bombers in Suffolk, I got a bad feeling about him. Nothing about him appeared trustworthy, and rather than being approached, it seemed he was the one setting up a deal. I had memories of Baakza and felt this was another case of an agent provocateur. He had initially claimed the people who approached him wanted to bring ten kilos of amphetamines from the Netherlands into Eye but then it changed to ten kilos of cannabis. That didn't make it a big enough case for us, so I passed it to the local collection.

What didn't help his cause was the fact he kept paging me all the time. One Sunday night, I came out of the cinema to find he'd been trying to contact me. When I didn't reply, he contacted the boss and complained. I was glad to see the back of him.

That's what we were up against with informants. Therefore, despite the huge resources we threw at it, the Isle of Wight job turned into a big waste of time. I ended up staying there for six weeks, stuck with a strange cast of characters – many of them good, but some others who could only be described as eccentric.

| | |

Customs might not have had the same culture of law-breaking corruption as the police, but we had our share of problem cases. We were also prone to the odd security lapse, which, had news got out, would have definitely embarrassed the service.

For instance, a consignment of 50 new computers was once delivered to Custom House. One of the security guards at the entrance gate, on a walkie-talkie, passed a message to the admin office inside, letting them know they had arrived. They said they'd come down after lunch to collect them. In the meantime, a gang of thieves who were scanning the radio traffic on the nearby streets turned up with a small lorry and stole all the computers from the Custom House front door.

It was known that criminals watched the car park and noted the makes and registrations of vehicles so they would know if they were being followed, yet the bosses and officers persisted in parking surveillance cars there.

I was surprised the Batmobile wasn't stolen when it appeared, out of the blue, on the quay of Custom House where seized vehicles were also parked. The iconic car, from the 1960s *Batman* TV series, starring Adam West, must have been seized over an import duty issue, and just sat there, in full view of the public.

Goods were being seized all the time – especially drugs. That constant smell of marijuana indicated there was probably a hundred tonnes of gear stored on the premises, worth billions. One of those tonnes might well have been a consignment we seized from a notorious smuggler, who up until then had managed to evade justice. Four times he had appeared in court and four times he was acquitted. I was tasked to carry out some surveillance on the house he shared with a famous actress in Surrey. It was a large mansion, so I parked up a couple of miles away, intending to walk past the property to look less conspicuous. As I strolled down the road a flash Jaguar pulled over. I looked over and couldn't believe it. Driving the car was the actress. Surely I hadn't been spotted?

'Do you want a lift?' she asked, after winding down the window.

'No, thanks,' I said, trying to think on my feet. 'I'm on my way to meet a friend.'

She shrugged and drove off.

I carried on past the house but, given what happened, couldn't hang about. It was only years later that I read an article on the actress which revealed she used to cruise around picking up strangers in her car. Was that what she was doing when I met her?

I don't believe the case against her partner succeeded. A reason why might have been something a colleague who arrested him found in his diary. There was a listing for 'Dan the jury man', with a telephone number. Was he the go-to guy to nobble juries? After what happened previously with the IRA smugglers I had every reason to think so.

|||

I spent eighteen months with the boat team and, while there was a frustration that a lot of the operations didn't come off, I had already quickly made my mind up that it wasn't for me.

Over the first few summer months, when I had been spending a lot of time on the Devon coast, carrying out surveillance or being on standby to assist our undercover sailor, it was perfectly pleasant, if unrewarding. But as time went on and I spent long winters in the freezing cold watching for importations that never seemed to come off, it was a long slog. And most of my Drugs J colleagues had neither the intellect nor humour of my money teammates.

As we entered 1993, what confirmed it for me was a job at Felixstowe. A container arrived with a shipment of cannabis inside we estimated was worth £1 million. We put a tracking device on it and watched to see who would come and claim it. Nobody did. So, we kept watching, around the clock. I spent long, tiresome, twelve-hour shifts staring at a container. The weeks went on and still nobody claimed their shipment.

I had started a night course for a diploma in Management and went once a week to Birkbeck College, part of the University of London. Working for the Juliets gave me lots of time to look over my notes on accounting. Whiling away the hours, sitting outside a house or watching a boat or container, I became an expert on LIFO (Last-In, First-Out) and FIFO (First-In, First-Out) stocktaking. It was a four-year course, which would eventually lead to an MBA. I hoped not all of those years would be spent sitting on the coast staring at boxes.

I ended up spending six weeks at Felixstowe. It was mind-numbing stuff. Nobody ever came to claim their cannabis. It became clear the port had the usual rip off team, which was becoming an ever-increasing problem. Somebody must've tipped them off, otherwise why would you just abandon a million quid's worth of dope?

It was the same story everywhere. Working on the coast I saw first-hand that, despite our best efforts to thwart the drug smugglers, it was a never-ending tide. It didn't matter what steps we took, the importers found a way to circumvent them. It was estimated that we seized less than 10 per cent of illegal drugs imported. And we were always hearing of new, and unexpected, ways drugs were being brought in.

Through the Romeos, the DLO in Brazil passed on intelligence that diplomats there were bringing in cocaine in their diplomatic bags. It was so brazen. They gave us the name of one suspect at the Brazilian embassy. Needing foot soldiers, they asked I assist, and we followed him to see what he was doing and who his associates were. I tailed him after he finished work one night and followed him towards Putney Bridge. When he ducked down onto the tow path by the river I thought we were getting somewhere. He met a younger man who was waiting in the shadows. Could this be one of his distributors? I followed them both a little further on. They ducked down under a bridge and when I got a bit closer I realised he was just cruising for sex. We didn't manage to find evidence of any wider drugs network.

I started to question why we even bothered. I wasn't alone. Within Customs, many knew the drugs war was futile and some senior officers debated the merits of the prohibition policy and whether it would be better if the government legalised the trade and taxed it. I could see their point. Nothing we did made any difference. Even when we did manage to seize tonnes of cocaine, the street price never changed. Surely it was better to control the trade, to monitor purity and hygiene, and remove thousands and thousands from the criminal justice system?

The more I saw the more I came to realise the government's heavy-handed approach was simply a political PR exercise. It was a waste of time, little more than an industry to keep police and Customs going. The Treasury argued that if you legalised drugs and taxed their use people would still smuggle it, like they did tobacco, but the truth was they didn't want to be seen to be going soft on the traffickers and junkies. For years they had been saying what a scourge on society it was and how they were winning the war on drugs. That's why Customs bosses loved the documentaries on the service and encouraged our cooperation, and why any big seizures were celebrated with photos of the haul circulated around newspapers. Trumpeting our successes led to more money and greater assets, and so it went on. It was like a game. We threw more resources at a problem and the importers came up with ways to stay ahead.

The perfect example was on the seas. It didn't matter how many cutters we had, we couldn't keep with the RIBs flying across the channel or up from Morocco. We could never catch them.

It occurred to me that we only seemed to catch the crap criminals. We could be at Euston Station following a target that Alpha told us should be on the 10.30am to Lime Street to meet some Scouse smack smuggler. More than once, we watched as our target struggled to navigate British Rail before privatisation, and boarded a train to Birmingham New Street, or somewhere else instead. Sometimes I felt like tapping the target on the shoulder and saying, 'It's that one, on platform 15.'

It didn't help that my personal circumstances had changed. When I'd first put down my preference to join the Juliets I was single and eager to throw myself into a new challenge. It had taken several months to move and then a year further down the line I was in a relationship, feeling fairly settled and my priorities had changed.

Charmian and I had moved to Hampstead by then, and we were having a fantastic time in this beautiful area. With a combined annual salary of £47,000, we bought our flat for £97,000. That same flat now would cost over a million. Our neighbours included the former Labour leader Michael Foot and fellow

Sheffielder Michael Palin, who I would sometimes meet while jogging on the heath and we'd discuss the latest travails affecting our beloved Wednesday. In the evenings, world-renowned Marxist historian Eric Hobsbawm would be in the Magdala pub down the road, made famous by Ruth Ellis, the last lady to be hanged in the UK. Our local library held monthly talks by figures like John le Carré, *Rumpole Of The Bailey*-creator John Mortimer and Martin Amis, while the Screen on the Hill cinema held local film premieres, such as Louis Malle's *Damage,* which the great director attended. Hampstead was an eclectic cultural mix in the early nineties. In the Louis Viennese café, you could be chatting one minute to an acclaimed playwright and the next a Jewish concentration camp survivor, with their identification number tattoo clearly visible on their forearm. It was a lovely place to live. From May to October, I'd swim in the ponds on the Heath and, after spending long days and weeks on the coast, I yearned to get back home there.

Long before I had climbed aboard the cutter, I questioned my decision to join this team. It hadn't been quite what I expected. I knew drug work was 90 per cent surveillance, but at least on the money teams there was a chance you might be stuck in the City or a nice part of London, near home. Now, I was spending most of my time at the ports, with colleagues I had little in common with.

Also, the ID was about to change. As a bulwark against encroachment from other agencies, it was decided that all local Collection Investigation Units would amalgamate with us, to form a new National Investigation Service (NIS), some 3,000 strong.

In response to this, and by the time I made up my mind to leave, an internal advert came round in the local circular for a job focusing on strategic intelligence, which I thought would be interesting during these changing times and that might be a better fit for me.

While tactical intelligence dealt with the here and now, like an imminent importation of heroin from Pakistan on a flight the following morning, strategic intelligence looked at the bigger picture, the trends that were happening in the drug or fraud worlds.

It would involve closer cooperation with the spooks and GCHQ – without any need to get my feet wet.

CHAPTER 17

||||||||||||||||||||||||||||||||||||||||||

Trendsetters

'You asked for any unusual seizures?' the officer at Harwich said. 'Well, you might want to come down and have a look at this.'

After my last experience of nearby Felixstowe, also in East Anglia Collection, I did think, this better be good. I wasn't disappointed. Following a tip from an informant, Customs in Suffolk had been on the lookout for a silver Mercedes. Given Harwich was one of the busiest passenger ports in the country, even finding the right car wouldn't have been easy. Expecting there to be cocaine stashed inside the body of the car, they started stripping it. Two days later they found what they were looking for – two kilos of coke hidden in the wishbone. For this, the £50,000 car had to be stripped to a virtual skeleton.

I didn't know what the wishbone of a car was, or even looked like, before I went down there. I now know it's part of the steering mechanism, connecting the front wheel with the car's chassis. It's a massive component made of welded metal. How someone even thought to stash drugs there was anyone's guess, but they must have thought that no one would ever find it.

It was exactly the response we were looking for when we asked the regional collections to let us know of any unusual seizures of illegal drugs or any illicit items, concealments, passenger or freight routings or fraud trends. This could range from arms to booze and fags, from biological material to endangered wildlife, the whole gambit that Customs controlled.

When it came to light, no one had ever heard of the wishbone concealment before. We analysed the reports and photographs, then sent out a Threat Assessment with full related details and pictures to all Collections for dissemination to their local officers. Two months later, Dover Collection got in touch. They had found the same thing – this time it was a kilo of cocaine, also concealed in the wishbone. Clearly, we had the makings of a new trend on our hands. This was precisely the role of Strategic Intelligence, and a great start for the newly formed team.

Every day there could be as many as eight drug seizures around the coast and at airports, container bases or in the post. In fact, we had a permanent Customs team at the massive Mount Pleasant Sorting Office, in Holborn, which dealt with most of the foreign post. They had the most sickening seizures to deal with, from child pornography to degenerates who sent packages of their own excrement to each other. When Customs colleagues raided the recipients' homes they'd find piles neatly packed in the fridges, ready to use. The National Coordination Unit (NCU) received a report for each one. We analysed the seizure records every day, checking any names on CEDRIC, the PNC, with known contacts, previous convictions, location and method. Even the smallest drugs seizures were plotted on a map, to try to find patterns and identify clusters of couriers.

Then we worked with the operational drug and other front-line teams and the local collections, to alert staff and managers for policy implications to help inform their work. For serial drugs seizures, our local colleagues would then work with police to try to determine who was behind these new clusters.

For instance, if we found five seizures from couriers in different locations around the UK, but they all came from Edinburgh, we could assume they were probably all working for the same organiser. We would feed this out to Customs and police north of the border, to help find out who was behind them.

We split the eighteen regional collections among the team. I had four I visited regularly, including East Midlands, which I asked for as it included Sheffield. I got to travel around the country, and I was no longer spending time just staring at a container. I would also visit the operational staff for fraud trends in the VAT and Excise offices, and we encouraged them to report anything unusual.

Sport utility vehicles (SUVs) were becoming increasingly popular, and while I was in Glasgow – another of my collections – I asked one of the VAT officers if there was anything going on with them we should know about.

'Funnily enough,' he said. 'We've got a local dealer for one of the big Japanese manufacturers. He's also the approved repair and service centre for them. He came to see us and said he'd noticed something strange. He has sole concession for west of Scotland, but it was capped at 50 cars annually and he knows all the customers he has sold to. He said he'd had eight SUVs to service in the last month from people he didn't know. This shouldn't be the case, given the numbers sold in the area.'

We discovered the SUVs were coming into Hamburg, which had enjoyed unusual status as a free port since 1888, which meant imported goods could be stored there without Customs duties. We learned that a criminal gang was stealing the cars from Hamburg, and they were turning up in Scotland. The dealer knew he hadn't sold the cars brought to his workshop. This was of concern from a VAT and import duty angle.

For any trends we considered urgent, especially when it came to drugs, we could post a threat assessment in an hour, but for something like this we would publish it in our monthly magazine for all frontline staff.

When we visited the collections, we also trained the local intelligence staff in mobile on-foot surveillance techniques and other tradecraft, to better standardise the skillset across the country. The only difference was they weren't trained to do pursuit driving.

Our team had much closer links to MI6 and GCHQ now, and I liaised with Annie Machon at MI5, before she and her boyfriend and fellow intelligence officer, David Shayler, blew the whistle on a series of alleged crimes committed by the service. I found her really helpful and during a tour she gave me of Century House, MI5's new HQ, she came across as intelligent and principled.

The agencies provided the latest relevant intelligence from their counterparts around the world. The CIA in America might have information from human or technical intelligence that a particular new method of concealment was now favoured, or a new supply route had started up from a country not previously considered a transit area for cocaine. They also provided a lot of information about what we called strategic exports, or arms smuggling.

All the information we collated, including daily drug seizures, went to the NCU, which included Control, who managed all the ID operations 24-hours-a-day, and was part of our intelligence branch. Each collection had a Collection Coordination

Unit (CCU) that managed all operations on a local level. Some of these were not 24-hour and were covered by Control overnight. The NCU was expanding into the collections, something many were in favour of. In the collections, only each CCU had access to CEDRIC, whereas in the ID, every team had at least one terminal with access.

We didn't just analyse drug trends, we also looked at fraud. The VAT offices wanted access to financial disclosures from the banks. When somebody paid in a large sum in cash, there was a high chance it was a VAT or other tax fraud. There was potentially valuable intelligence in it for them, but the problem for the tax investigators was the money laundering legislation fell under the Drug Trafficking Act, so they couldn't access the information. We sought to remedy that by providing the link between the operational drug teams, DFIB and the fraud units.

We also provided a link to the intelligence services, for anything that wasn't a live operation. Positive vetting was the term we used for liaising with the spooks, and our dealings were everything you would expect. Collectively, we referred to them as 'Box', due to their addresses at the time – MI6 was Box 850, while MI5 was Box 500.

Our MI6 contact was typically posh, Oxbridge-educated, with a double-barrelled surname. He provided us with international trends and non-specific intelligence that we would disseminate to the frontline. It always felt like he was doing us a huge favour by speaking to us. I likened the relationships we had with 'five' and 'six' to the ones we had with barristers and solicitors.

Annie Machon introduced us to the spook who ran things in Northern Ireland – a very stressful brief during the Troubles. He was probably the ideal spy chief; standing at just five-foot-four-inches tall, bald, with standard NHS glasses, he was the last person you'd suspect.

For all their cooperation with us, there was a bigger play happening. MI6 wanted to take over all our foreign work and put Customs under their remit. Internationally, it wouldn't take that much of a leap to make it happen. In places like Bogota, in Colombia, there was an MI6 station, but two or three Customs people were already operating out of there. It was a dilemma for Customs hierarchy. They needed the intelligence, but not at the expense of our autonomy.

While we worked alongside them, however, it was fascinating to watch how they operated. At the time, mobile phone technology was moving on from analogue to digital. The security of phone calls had been a hot topic ever since Princess Diana was caught by a scanner in conversation with her close friend James Gilbey, the heir to a gin company, and the transcripts were published in the *Sun*. The fallout from 'Squidgygate' – as the paper dubbed it, after Gilbey's affectionate nickname for the princess – and 'Camillagate', when Prince Charles was also caught engaging in explicit conversation with his mistress, Camilla Parker Bowles, had put the spotlight on MI5, when technical analysis of the tape concluded it had been doctored and suggested Diana's call couldn't have been picked up by a scanner at the time of the call due to the distance between the phone and the scanner, which suggested it had been leaked at a later date precisely to embarrass her. The scandals, however, brought into sharp focus how easy it was to eavesdrop into mobile phone calls.

The intelligence services put a story out that digital mobile phones were far more secure than analogue, and couldn't be hacked. Of course, it was nonsense. Digital calls were just as susceptible. The story had the desired effect. Criminals immediately switched to digital phones, and we were able to gather as much intelligence and evidence as before. It was a classic disinformation campaign. Indeed, we'd previously struggled with some criminals who guessed it took two weeks to get an intercept warrant. We'd follow them and at the end of each fortnight they'd dump their mobile in the Thames or local river or reservoir.

One of the best things we initiated was use of a software programme designed by a Cambridge company called i2, through which you could scan documents to link every movement and action in a suspected criminal enterprise.

We bought the licence and kept it in the NCU, where a team of three dedicated intelligence officers, led by a female officer poached from Scotland Yard, did the analysis. It was an extremely valuable tool, and eventually we bought more packages and licences for all NIS teams and frontline offices throughout the outfield, which was anything outside the HQ.

Its operational usefulness was tested by the Romeos on the Curtis Warren case. Everything was scanned in to the i2 – every suspect, every call made, every phone number from call logs, all financial transactions and any movements we'd monitored. There were scores of defendants, and details for every single one were added. On that one case alone, there were several hundred-thousand calls and transactions between suspects. When the Romeos surveyed the analysis they said if they'd had that before the arrests were made they could have rounded up about six more people. We were involved with the programme from its first development, and its success eventually saw it rolled out to law enforcement throughout the world.

Unfortunately, for all the progress we were making with intelligence, we didn't have a programme that could weed out the bad apples in our own service. I had an ominous feeling as soon as an officer called Peter Hawkins joined us from Gatwick. He was a twenty-stone walrus and, curiously, had been privately educated at a posh school in Newcastle, which I thought took some doing in those days. I could tell what he was like from the moment he started, as he was throwing his considerable weight around. He struck me as an obnoxious bully.

My first words to him were: 'If you try to fuck me, I'm going to finish you.'

From that moment on we had an understanding. I watched him rub people up the wrong way, but he didn't try anything with me and, in fact, we started to get on.

He had only been with us for nine months when we got a call from the police in Sussex. 'You've got a Customs officer called Peter Hawkins?' the cop said.

'Yes.'

'He's got a house at Gatwick he rents out to anyone wanting to stay local. A woman has complained because he drilled a spy hole to watch her in the shower. There's a hole in his wardrobe that leads to the wall that leads to the bathroom.'

The police were informing us, rather than simply arresting him, because they said there was nothing they could charge him with. As it was in the privacy of his own home, it was not actually a crime.

As with most offices, as soon as word got round, the first thing we did was nickname him 'Peeping Pete'. We did, however, have a problem. What do you do with someone who is clearly a menace but isn't facing criminal charges? The bosses confronted Hawkins, believing the only sensible option was to sack him. However, once he realised why he was being disciplined, he produced a little black book, detailing every time a colleague, junior or senior, had done anything dodgy or unethical, threatening to go public should he lose his job. It wasn't surprising, therefore, when they decided not to sack him and, instead, moved him to the West Country Collection, where it was hoped he wouldn't do more damage.

This happened quite a lot. There was a case of an officer on a rummage team – who scoured vast ships for drug consignments – down on the south coast who had a drink problem. The situation came to a head when he was so intoxicated he fell overboard into the harbour while searching a boat. For everyone's safety, not least his own, he was moved to a VAT office inland. That was a standard policy for anyone on an ID team that messed up – they were moved to a VAT office.

In 1995, after two years on strategic intelligence, I was once again itching for a fresh challenge as I hadn't been put forward for promotion, which I felt I'd deserved. The rules at the time meant you could only promote one person at a time due to budgeting, and my boss chose to promote my colleague who she'd previously worked with, so there was an air of favouritism about it.

Then, I discovered a Customs team whose work interested me. During an NCU conference I met with officers from Customs D – the commercial fraud team that dealt with breaches of the EU's Common Agricultural Policy (CAP). I hadn't known it existed but discovered it was one of the few teams that went up against the big multinational food companies that imported into Europe.

I spoke to Richard Vallance, a senior case officer, who explained the team worked mainly for the European Commission because, since 1992, the import duties and quotas were set for the whole of Europe, not the individual member states. They worked on behalf of UCLAF, the Anti-Fraud Coordination Unit based in Brussels where some Customs D staff were seconded.

He told me about an interesting case he was working on against Heinz foods. They had been flouting EU law and he had the power to act. My ears pricked up. For a long time, I'd grown frustrated that big businesses were able to routinely break tax laws with virtual impunity and nobody wanted to take them on in court. Was this the team to do it?

CHAPTER 18

The fruit and veg team

In the Scombridae fish family, tuna and bonito share many similarities. They look the same, behave the same and, most importantly, taste pretty much the same. Nobody, apart from perhaps a professor of agriculture, could tell the difference between them.

One crucial area where they did differ, Richard Vallance explained, was how they were taxed by the EU. The import duty on tuna, depending on whether it was fresh, prepared or frozen, ranged between 18 to 24 per cent. For bonito, it was 7.5 per cent.

When you looked at the import stats, he said, hardly any tuna was imported to the EU compared to a bonanza of bonito. Yet, on the supermarket shelves, tuna appeared to be in far more plentiful supply. Put simply, he said, fish was being imported as bonito and sold as tuna.

He suspected Heinz, the well-known multinational food company responsible for Ketchup and baked beans, of this very practice. If they were taking advantage of cheaper tariffs, by falsely declaring tuna as bonito, then they were committing a crime.

Under section 152 of the Customs and Excise Management Act 1979, Customs had the power to compound offences. This meant they could stop or stay any offence, taking back any charges levied against an accused. Its power was far-reaching. Even if someone was convicted of drug trafficking, Customs could release them from prison, without recourse to a judge. When it came to big businesses, this was a very useful tool. Rather than prosecute, which could mean a lengthy lottery in a law court and the expenses associated with it, there was the option of compounding the offence. The company avoided going to court and the negative publicity that would come with it, but they accepted responsibility and paid a fine. Significantly, national authorities, like Customs, kept such penalties for themselves, unlike import duties that went into the EU's coffers. If the fine was not a material amount, the firm might also be able to hide it from auditors and shareholders. It was the same for famous or powerful individuals and meant a much easier life for the Customs officers and their timid bosses, because they didn't have a potentially lengthy and complicated prosecution to deal with.

'We're going to comp them,' Richard said. That was how Customs termed it. He said he was going to go to Pittsburgh, Pennsylvania, where Heinz had its headquarters, to interview its directors and take statements. If Heinz agreed to the compounding, they would pay the £1-million duty they owed, and the penalty Customs imposed.

'We've worked it out at 57 per cent,' Richard said, with a smile. Heinz's labels famously referred to '57 varieties'. Although largely a made-up number – dating back to when company founder Henry John Heinz, who was looking for ways to market his food business in 1896, spotted an advert for '21 varieties of shoes' in New York and liked the idea of pegging a number to his product – the Heinz company did assign 57 products to a list of the varieties in 1924. The classic tomato ketchup was listed at number 48 on the list, with number one being baked beans with pork and tomato sauce.

If Heinz paid the tax and the penalty, Customs agreed not to prosecute or publicise the misdemeanour but, if asked about it, they would not deny it.

Richard explained that nearly every FTSE 100 company had been compounded at one stage. One of the most famous cases was Virgin, owned by Richard Branson. In 1971, when he was still a young, budding entrepreneur, his record shop in Oxford Street, London, was losing money. To dig himself out of debt, Branson tried to avoid paying purchase taxes, by pretending to export albums that Virgin sold in Britain. In the UK at the time, music retailers paid a heavy 33 per cent levy on records sold domestically, but the tax didn't apply to vinyl shipped abroad. While attempting to drive a large shipment of discs to Belgium, Branson discovered that he could stop at Customs in Dover, get his export paperwork stamped, then bring the cargo back to sell at home, where he could pocket the tax savings. This is what was known as a carousel fraud. Customs began investigating Virgin's export forms after an employee at the record label EMI questioned Branson's low record prices. They then noticed that Branson claimed to have exported 30,000 records inside a single Land Rover.

To confirm the scam, Customs marked EMI records that Branson was officially buying to export using an ultraviolet pen. They then placed orders for the same records through Virgin's mail order service. When the marked merchandise arrived in their mailboxes, it proved they weren't being exported.

Branson realised the ruse and tried to put the marked stock on the racks at his Oxford Street store, to be sold there instead, not realising that Customs had greater search powers than even the police. Customs raided his shop and Branson spent a night in jail, before his mother paid bail. In the deal offered to Branson, he could pay £60,000 (the equivalent of more than £700,000 in today's money). If he couldn't pay, he would be re-arrested and put on trial.

He had to pay it immediately, but Branson has said that he spent the next two years ploughing every penny of the cash generated from his shops into expanding the business to pay off the debt he incurred paying off his bill to Customs.

Branson was certainly not the only famous face who avoided paying his taxes. There was a rule – two strikes and you're out. Companies could be compounded once, but if they did it again, policy stated they would be prosecuted. They also must admit to the offence.

The more I heard about the remit of the commercial fraud teams the more I wanted to join one. However, when I mentioned it to senior officer Roger Mills – he was the undercover officer who had lost £250,000 on a drug importation – he said, 'What do you want to join the fruit and veg team for?'

That's what it was disparagingly known as within the operational drugs teams – that, or the greengrocers. In the eyes of some officers, it perhaps sounded less exciting than following drugs around the world, but I liked the sound of Customs taking on big businesses, making them pay.

My stint on Strategic Intelligence had seen me fitted once again for promotion but still it hadn't happened due to budget constraints. I admit, another part of the allure of Customs D was that it might be a chance for me to make my name. And so, in 1995, I moved over to the commercial fraud branch.

My boss Nick Gallacher, the SIO, was a likeable chap from Manchester and a City fan before the mega money arrived. The team was a welcoming and harmonious bunch, and there were no tensions from drugs busts going wrong to cause issues. Although I was still a junior investigator, I was one of the more experienced people there.

I spent my first few weeks making regular trips to Brussels, preparing for a forthcoming investigation into tuna imports from Turkey, on behalf of UCLAF. We were invited as representatives from one of seven countries involved.

It was a very civilised existence. We travelled first class on the Eurostar to Brussels, for a few days or occasionally for the whole week, and enjoyed the benefits of a tax-free supermarket in the office basement that staff were able to shop in. We met Customs officers from other countries as they were all based in the same office.

I was interested to learn of the various commercial fraud issues faced by the EU. The importation of rice was a big problem because it was subject to high taxes. There were loopholes, however. Producers who took it to be milled in the Netherlands Antilles, in the Caribbean, could bring it in for free because those territories were subject to the same agreement the Dutch had when it joined the EU. The only trouble was that when you went to the Antilles there were no mills. Producers who said they milled it there clearly hadn't.

There were other issues to do with tuna. If it was from Ecuador it could be brought in duty-free, because the European Union had deals with 'most favoured nations', designed to help the economies of developing nations. A way of qualifying for Ecuadorian status was if a ship had 60 per cent or more of its crew from there and it was registered in Ecuador. Going by the number of vessels that came to be from Ecuador, the country had some sized shipping fleet. There were all sorts of scams in operation – and they always involved massive amounts of money.

Richard completed his case against Heinz, and as expected they agreed to be compounded in return for paying the £1.57-million penalty and import duty owed. For the 'fruit and veg' team it was a big result against a large company, But I couldn't help noticing that they hadn't yet prosecuted a major firm found to be flouting tax laws. Nor had anyone else. That was all about to change.

CHAPTER 19

||||||||||||||||||||||||||||||||||||||||||||

Doing my duty

When Nia Jones, a bright, young, Welsh trader control officer at the Swindon Excise office, contacted Anchor Foods to say she wanted to arrange a date to undertake an inspection at their local factory and offices, the response should have been routine. For a major trader like Anchor, the wholly owned UK subsidiary of the New Zealand Dairy Board, famous for its spreadable butter, it should have been subjected to, at least, an annual 'control', or inspection visit. Under the Conservative government's policy of trader self-control, however, such visits had slipped to whenever the reduced staffing levels allowed, which could be several years, unless the firm had a poor compliance record.

Anchor Foods had two key sites in England – the factory in Swindon, where it employed around 400 staff, and New Zealand Dairy Board's UK headquarters in Reigate, Surrey, which housed about 30 staff.

Anchor told Nia she was welcome to come to the factory for the inspection, and a date was set a couple of weeks hence. Two days later, however, Swindon Excise received a voluntary disclosure from Anchor Foods. By contacting Customs, Anchor were effectively saying, we've discovered a problem and we're telling you about it. Under the voluntary disclosure policy, companies that made such disclosures would not normally be punished criminally, because they were being up front and honest and notifying Customs of any mistakes or errors or extra tax to be paid. Such a declaration, however, must be unprompted.

The issues they wanted to raise were with their butter importations. Like other former global powers, when Britain joined the European Economic Community, as it was then, in 1973, they negotiated what were called accession benefits, so former colonies could carry on being able to export to Britain and Europe, even though import duties for goods arriving in Britain were now being handled by the EEC. The theory was that these countries would have ten years or so to diversify their economies. That was back in the early seventies, though, and this was now 1995.

Anchor wasn't just any company. The New Zealand Dairy Board was a farmers' cooperative, which amounted to a third of the country's economy. Ever since butter had been imported in by early British settlers, New Zealand had adopted it as its own. From the 19th century, butter was viewed not only as a basic food staple, loved for its rich flavour and appreciated as an energy source, but it was also seen as a valuable trading commodity from which the country could make vast profits. New Zealand butter and cheese became as treasured as gold or silver, and was so integral to the country's economy that, by the 1960s, the Dairy Board marketing campaign boasted how 'New Zealand is Butterland'. Butter accounted for 30 per cent of export earnings as far back as 1935. Since 1973, its annual quota for butter access to the EU was 52,000 tonnes but that had recently been increased to 76,767 tonnes. Given the amount of butter produced by European countries, most notably France with its powerful farming lobby, competition was fierce. To differentiate itself from the domestic market, Anchor had devised its spreadable butter, which had proved very popular in Britain.

The legislation stated that their annual quota of butter products must be made with butterfat between 80 and 82 per cent. Any butter below 80 per cent butterfat could not be labelled as such and above 82 per cent did not qualify for this preferential treatment. As the balance was mainly made up of salt and water, it was the butterfat Anchor were desperate for.

Against this backdrop, Nia Jones visited the Anchor factory to carry out her control. The company explained that there had been some recent imports where the butterfat was slightly higher than 82 per cent. They apologised and gave assurances it wouldn't happen again. They said the issue was minimal and offered to pay a few grand of the duty owed. Nia was suspicious and reported this back to her senior officer, who decided to notify the NIS.

The first we learned about it was when Swindon Excise called my boss, Nick. He relayed the story to me. As the last one in, I didn't yet have an ongoing investigation. I might have been making trips to Turkey, but that was an EU-wide probe that may not have led to a criminal case.

I called Nia and arranged to go to Swindon to meet her. Only nineteen, and diminutive in stature, at first glance she looked, ironically, like butter wouldn't melt in her mouth, but that belied her steely determination. Her enthusiasm and scepticism of the official line reminded me of myself back in Salford. I respected her and her senior officer for sensing it could be something bigger and bringing it to our attention.

She gave me the full details of her dealings with Anchor and, afterwards, I chatted it over with her boss. Their voluntary disclosure timing was clearly only prompted by Nia's notice of a control visit.

'I don't believe them,' I said.

'Neither do we,' they said.

I went back to the office, with the intention of talking over what to do, but already I was thinking this merited further research and maybe an aggressive raid with a search warrant to establish if Anchor were telling the truth. Were the slip-ups a couple of blips, or was this a long-standing and wider issue?

My thoughts went back to that initial Revenue Awareness course when I first joined Customs, and what we had been told by the senior investigator: everybody's bent.

'I think we should raid them,' I said to Nick, after I'd made some further enquiries and we'd had a discussion. To me, it was simple. The fact the disclosure had come a day or two after Nia's approach was highly suspect. Even if the company were being honest and had only just noticed a couple of small mistakes, then we'd go in there, establish the facts and we'd recover whatever they owed in unpaid duty. I didn't see it as a big deal, but the justification was there for us to act. Either way, we couldn't lose.

I was aware, though, how big a deal it would be to request a search warrant against a powerful branded company with a state behind them. Not only that, but we would also need to target the New Zealand Dairy Board office in Reigate. Persuading a judge to give us a search warrant might not be easy, because when people start seeing famous names, they know how quickly a case can become high profile, which means more is at risk if it falls apart. It was one thing to tap the local Chinese or Indian restaurant, but to take on a company that was essentially one third of a state's economy was serious stuff.

I got the feeling Nick would have preferred to ask the firm for related papers, pay them a visit, look over the documentation and then assess the situation. I was adamant, though.

'If the documentation is all in order, then fine. It's going to confirm their story. But, if not, that's all we're going to get because they're not going to let us see anything that might incriminate them,' I argued.

Apart from his career, what I think worried Nick was that there was no precedent. There had been no previous commercial raids like this, that I knew of. He knew Anchor would have a team of top lawyers, and we could be inviting an almighty shitstorm.

When I thought back to the cigarette warehouse near Sheffield, the investigators did not have a warrant and the company refused to fully cooperate until the ID agents used nefarious means. As HM Customs, we had a right to those documents. We had the power to get anything we wanted, but only a warrant would guarantee we got everything required. A company could hand over all manner of documents relating to imports and exports, but, on an enquiry visit, they were not going to give you vital internal emails related to trading and taxes, which was where the crucial evidence would be.

While Nick was reluctant, we consulted with the Assistant Chief Investigation Officer, Cedric Andrews, who oversaw the whole branch and had done for some years. He was well respected and dealt with intelligence chiefs and the Customs board daily. His branch had been involved in the Iraq 'Supergun' affair, when Customs probed two businesses, one of them Sheffield Forgemasters, for selling long range weapons to Iraq. The scandal led to government ministers being accused of letting businessmen be wrongly convicted rather than tell how much they knew about the arms trade with Saddam Hussein's regime. The same branch was also involved in the Matrix Churchill affair. The Scott inquiry into the scandal was still to publish its report when I joined the fruit and veg team.

Given the fallout that ensued from those two scandals that he had to deal with, it was understandable that Cedric had reservations about taking on something so high profile. However, I managed to convince Nick and Cedric of the case's merits. Eventually, they agreed, and said okay, let's go for it.

Feeling vindicated, I began putting together an operational plan. We needed to target both sites at the same time. I imagined that most of the decisions would be taken at the Dairy Board office in Reigate – where we had done some drive-bys – but there could be valuable evidence in the factory offices too, especially as it was where the imports clerk worked. I also figured Swindon staff would be more upfront than the highly paid executives and managers in Reigate. This factory was in England's 'Silicon Valley', not some deprived former mining area.

When I tried to picture a best-case scenario, I thought we might be talking about recovering up to £300,000 or so in unpaid duty – which, plus penalties, would have represented a decent result.

I drafted the request for the search warrants, which, as usual, we went to court to have signed. Any fears I might have had that the judge would baulk at taking on such a large firm were unfounded.

We now had our raid warrants. It was time to discover the scale of what we were dealing with.

CHAPTER 20

||||||||||||||||||||||||||||||||||||||||||||||||||||

The raid

We gave them time to start their day, get settled, have a coffee. This wasn't like a drugs bust, when the element of surprise was crucial and the goal was to catch the criminals as early as possible with much noise and chaos to disorientate and confuse. We weren't going to arrest anybody. We were just looking for some documents and computer records.

I went down to Reigate with the main party, and a few of my colleagues and the local Swindon officers went to the factory. Our remit was quite restricted; we were only looking for anything related to Anchor's Customs import declarations. We weren't looking for any other tax irregularities.

Shortly after 9am, we announced our arrival and why we were there. It was a shared office block and the New Zealand Dairy Board occupied one floor. Not all the senior executives were present, but those that were looked stunned. Their expressions reminded me of the shock felt in Sheffield when the cigarette plant was raided. There was no resistance, but possibly some relief when we declared we were just there to conduct a search. We weren't going to be arresting anybody ... yet.

While the team began its work, I stood back. I didn't want to seize documents because that would deflect from my role as case officer. Nor did I want to be preoccupied with properly logging where documents were found, because that would then form the basis of my future witness statement. Most of my colleagues were very experienced, and I could trust them to do a good job. Operationally, I wanted to do as little as possible, so I could grasp the bigger picture.

Over in Swindon, Nia had conducted her arranged visit before this search. The company had shown her evidence of a few discrepancies. Now was the chance to see if that was the extent of the issue.

The New Zealand Dairy Board office was a hive of industry as officers meticulously poured over each piece of paperwork, making sure they didn't miss anything relevant to our investigation. Not long after we arrived, a colleague, Julia, approached me with some documents she had found relating to past imports. There was one she was keen for me to see. It was an internal email, copied to the New Zealand Dairy Board in Wellington. Attached to the email were the results of the butter testing at the Board in New Zealand, prior to its export, and then faxed to Reigate while the ship was in transit, before any declarations to Customs. This applied to scores of previous consignments. A large percentage of the results were above the 82 per cent butterfat limit.

I couldn't believe it. You couldn't get better evidence than that. It was a fantastic find.

Then a senior officer, Geoff, who I knew from his time on Drugs K, came to me with a file marked 'Legal'. In it, letters were written to the board's lawyers, a large, prestigious City firm with an army of tax solicitors. The letters gave a full background to the exportations and contained copies of some the butter test results, including those consignments at 84 per cent butterfat. It asked the question what they should do, as a ship was already in transit. The advice from the lawyers was unequivocal. Whatever exports did not meet Customs legislation were not permitted to be brought into the EU under the quota.

It was another startling piece of evidence – they had clearly chosen to ignore their own legal advice. As usual, the note, later copied to other executives here and in New Zealand, was subject to legal privilege and stamped accordingly, so it was questionable whether we would be allowed to use it in our case against them. However, it provided us with useful knowledge which we could use when interviewing the executives. Geoff asked me what I wanted to do.

'Bag it,' I replied, 'together with all the legal files.' He noted this on the property sheets and added it to the thousands of documents seized.

Within Customs law, there is what is called an absolute offence. This is crime without *mens rea*. It means you don't need to prove someone acted with a guilty mind. If you fill in your tax return and make a genuine mistake on a calculator, although you didn't mean to do it, it's still an untrue declaration. It is still an offence. The maximum sentence was two years in prison. A fraudulent declaration is one made knowingly, therefore with a guilty mind. The maximum sentence for each fraudulent declaration was seven years imprisonment, increasing for illegal drug importations.

As our investigators gathered up the mountain of paperwork, I felt relieved. The evidence we had uncovered fully justified my argument for a search warrant. I don't believe any of this would have been given to Nia voluntarily.

The most important thing when carrying out a search is recording accurately the chain of evidence, to note down precisely where and when material was found. As well as keeping a record for ourselves, we left them a copy. The more specific the information the better – the name of the employee's office, the location and description of the filing cabinet, the drawer in which it was found, the description on the file, the number for that document.

Not only did we scoop up all the documents we could find but I had also requested that the computer forensic team join us on the search. I knew that any files they could recover would be important. We needed to find out how long these declarations went back. The forensic team uplifted the computer records and the firm's back-up disc from the previous night. This was updated at the end of every working day.

In Swindon, while they didn't find anything quite as damning as the email Julia had, their job was made easier by the fact that Anchor had a clerk whose sole job was to handle all the Customs importation documentation and related records. They were all in the one place.

By around 4pm we loaded our haul into the boots and backseats of our cars. When we went back to Custom House everyone was cock-a-hoop. Nick was over the moon, and probably mightily relieved too. When they saw the key material, everyone was talking about the damning email. What we also had was advice from their lawyers, their test results and the knowledge that they still went ahead and made their declaration. We had an indication of the scale, which was suggesting hundreds of problematic imports were made, not the odd one or two. Technically, each fraudulent declaration carried its own prison sentence – and we were looking at potentially hundreds of declarations. Suddenly, this had all the hallmarks of a massive job, and we still had the material from Swindon to assess. I locked all the seized material up in the exhibits room, and that night we went to the pub. I was under no illusions of the scale of the work ahead – but we wanted to enjoy that moment.

The following day I began sifting through the documentation. As the case officer, I was handed all the material, and it was my responsibility to go through everything. This amounted to nearly 100,000 items.

We began meticulously matching up the declarations and the consignments with the results of what had been tested in New Zealand. We also poured over the email files to see if there was any more incriminating evidence.

I couldn't believe what we had unearthed. It was exhilarating. My first big investigation as a case officer could scarcely have gone any better so far. This was exactly what I wanted to do when I joined the commercial fraud branch. Finally, I could get my teeth into a big case, one that involved a large company and was intellectually challenging. Plus, it was complex, arcane law and struck at the heart of global trade policy and international relations.

Just when I started to think this might be the investigation that could really make my name, we hit a problem. A very big problem.

CHAPTER 21

|||||||||||||||||||||||||||||||||||||||

No, Minister

One week on from the raids, Nick called me: 'The Foreign Office wants to speak to us.'

'What do they want?' I asked.

'Don't know yet.'

While I didn't imagine it was to give us a pat on the back, I wasn't too concerned. From the evidence we'd seen so far, it was clear to me we were going to have to start arresting and interviewing people. There was more than enough to go on. The trail led all the way back to the New Zealand Dairy Board office in Wellington, from where there had been instructions from one senior executive on how they should proceed, with an admission they would be breaching EU regulations.

Two senior civil servants arrived at Custom House. They were of a grade far higher than anyone I'd ever met before. It was like something straight out of *Yes Minister*. They were archetypal Sir Humphrey Appleby types, assistant secretaries in charge of the New Zealand desk, in tailored pin-striped suits. Nick and I met with them. Their manner was terribly polite, but the message was clear: drop the investigation.

'Whatever you think you have, dear boy, it's our duty to inform you this has the potential to damage international relations,' one of them said. 'It will have all sorts of consequences.'

Not only would it harm our relationship with New Zealand, our Commonwealth cousins, but it also had the potential to cause ructions in the EU, they said. They told us to consider that it could have a detrimental impact on ordinary farmers over there, many of whom could well be British, or of British descent. Their other concern was that it would not help our friends in Europe either. They claimed the EU might use whatever evidence we had as an excuse to get rid of the New Zealand butter quota – something they had been trying to do for years, apparently.

'It would, therefore, be better for all concerned if this could just go away,' one said.

I wondered how they knew about it. Had someone in the New Zealand government contacted them? How high did this go? Whatever they had been told, they clearly had no idea of the strength of the evidence against the company already.

What they said about the EU was interesting. Since I'd worked with UCLAF (the Brussels-based Anti-Fraud Coordination Unit), I'd learned how powerful the French agricultural sector was. French farmers surely could not have been happy that Anchor was granted permission to sell so much butter in Europe. In my short time in Brussels, I'd seen that it was essentially the French who controlled the EU, effectively, with a very clever strategy. Every department had a director general and France supported a move to share the top jobs amongst the member states. UCLAF was known technically as DG21, for Director General 21. The French strategy was to give up all the head positions to other nations, but make sure their citizens held the deputy posts. It might look good to have the top job but, in practice, it's not the chief that does the work; they just do the politicking. It's the number twos that hold the power. In all the key posts, it was the French making the decisions. Also, their top public servants were chosen from the elite universities and had the best resources and training to promulgate premium policies. Take VAT for example, a French invention. This is the most efficient tax as its collected by traders with minimal state staff needed.

While import duties applied to all member states, there was no standardisation when it came to domestic taxes. You only had to look at the duty on alcohol and compare how cheap it was in France compared to the UK to see that. I could just imagine that if the French learned about the New Zealand Dairy Board flouting EU tax laws they would want to score political capital.

What had we unearthed – thanks to Nia's request for a control visit?

I left it to Nick to do the talking. He thanked the civil servants for their concern but told them: 'We don't know what we've got yet. We'll assess the evidence and keep in contact with you.'

What he said was strictly true. We had only reconciled a fraction of the documentation, but we already knew we had enough to potentially put some people in prison.

The Foreign Office weren't interested, however. This was just a major inconvenience to them. They just wanted to preserve the status quo and not rock the boat.

None of the senior Customs bosses joined us for the meeting and now I could see why. This was a career-defining case, whatever the outcome. If it was already causing ructions, who wanted to be associated with it before they were sure which way it would go?

Nick remained resolute and handled their request calmly. It was left that we would keep them informed of our progress.

Nick had been supportive throughout, but I felt like my spirits had gone from high to low in rapid-quick time. Here had come the suits to confirm everything I suspected about the public sector. If left to them, ultimately nothing would get done.

The more I thought about it, the more I realised that this case must be massive for people to have come to see us so quickly. It stiffened my resolve; I would keep going. I knew that unless I did something, this case would wither, because it required too much bottle and was too big for civil servants to handle. If the Sir Humphreys had their way, it would just be like it was with Heinz. We might get a penalty off them, but it would all be hushed up. I was determined not to let that happen. I hoped this interference would backfire against them.

We did two things after that meeting. First, we informed UCLAF, and I went to Brussels to visit our colleagues there and talk about what had been going on. They were responsive, but UCLAF have competing interests within their own unit – their job is to find fraud, and the EU's job is to have a competitive market and to protect their trading environment. So, while you might find a massive fraud, it could be of miniscule importance compared to a trading agreement.

The second thing I did was contact the European Court of Auditors in Luxembourg. They audit the European budget, to make sure taxpayers' money is being spent accordingly, so I knew they'd be interested. I found an ex-Customs investigator called John McDonald, who had moved to Luxembourg years ago. He was a very tenacious, experienced auditor, who travelled the world inspecting trade, tariffs and quotas for EU compliance.

As soon as I told him what was happening, he got very excited. He said the auditors had been unhappy about the Kiwis for years, as they had been having problems importing into other member states. He immediately made plans to come to London to look over some of the evidence. His enthusiasm was encouraging. It sounded like I'd found someone who understood what we had.

When John came to meet us, he brought with him a Danish colleague, Peter Larsen, who had also moved over from Customs. He provided great insight and knowledge, being from Aarhus, the home of MD Foods – the giant dairy company that made Lurpak butter, and one of Anchor's big customers. Nick joined me in the meeting.

I handed over copies of the damning email and legal material, with duplicates of hundreds of other documents seized, showing the massive scale of the issue.

As soon as John started reading, his face lit up. 'Look at the documents,' he said. 'Everything's here.'

He'd never seen anything like it.

'Brilliant work,' he said. 'They shouldn't even have this quota anyway.'

'What do you mean?' I asked.

He told me the history of the quota, about Britain's accession to the EEC and how that affected the colonies.

'They should have diversified their economies by now,' he said.

'What happened?'

'*Rainbow Warrior* happened.'

I remembered the bombing of the Greenpeace flagship in the Port of Auckland by two French foreign intelligence agents in 1985. The activists were on their way to protest a planned nuclear test in French Polynesia. A photographer drowned when the ship sank, and the bombing sparked international outrage.

John explained how, normally, the French would be the

most aggressive against the New Zealand Dairy Board quota, as their dairy farmers were a very powerful force. He told the story of how New Zealand police captured the two French agents and had them arrested for a range of offences, including arson and murder. However, a dirty deal was struck whereby the agents pleaded guilty to a reduced charge of manslaughter and were sentenced to ten years in prison. They were interned, not in a New Zealand jail but at a military base on the French Polynesian island of Hao. They only served two years there before being freed by the French government.

It was remarkably lenient for people convicted of manslaughter. John said the deal struck between the New Zealand and French governments meant that if France were to get back their agents, they had to agree not to oppose the butter quota during future trade negotiations. That's why, more than twenty years on from the formation of the EEC, New Zealand enjoyed an increased share of the European market. Suddenly, it made sense. The Foreign Office must have known this too. It was an international agreement, after all.

Incidentally, that same story about *Rainbow Warrior* and the background to the butter quota was confirmed to me by another source – an executive I later interviewed who used to work for Anchor, in Swindon. He also claimed the company was solely interested in butterfat and was short of this raw product because of their booming spreadable product and because they were limited by the quota.

'This is hundreds of millions of pounds worth of import duties,' John said, returning to the documents.

They were both amazed. We still had masses more material to sift through but already we could tell the quota breaches went back years.

John asked me for copies of the evidence. I was about to hand them over when Nick stopped me.

'It has to go through the legal process before we can give it to a foreign third party.'

I didn't agree. There was a process called *commission rogatoire*, by which foreign agencies could exchange material, but that was for formal proceedings like evidence in court. The auditors just wanted it for background at this stage.

Nick wanted to run it by the Solicitors' Office, but John and Peter needed to leave to catch their flight back to Luxembourg. I considered John a vital ally. His enthusiasm, plus the background information he divulged, convinced me it would be in our interests to involve him – so I gave him a copy of the relevant material. His knowledge and experience of complex EU trade and tax policy was beyond what anyone on our team had, plus he had a global view of events while we were more locally limited. I wasn't that worried. I couldn't see a problem with giving a European organisation documents that essentially related to EU importations. They didn't have the power to investigate matters of fraud, so didn't need it for evidence. If they uncovered something that concerned them, they were able to launch civil cases or pass it to UCLAF, but that was all.

Part of me was thinking it was natural justice. I felt it wouldn't do us any harm to expand it out and involve other bodies. If the Foreign Office was going to shut us down, perhaps someone else could pick up the ball and run with it. They might have been able to cause problems for Anchor and New Zealand in some other way. I'd also come to another conclusion. I wasn't going to be in the civil service forever. My reasons for joining the public sector in the first place were no longer relevant. I had a flat of my own, plus another property I jointly owned with

Charmian, so had a lucrative nest egg. Money was no longer a big issue. For me, having an inside toilet and bathroom was the height of luxury. I didn't need the security of a state pension, which most public sector staff hung on for, as property speculation gave me another source of income. I realised I had a skillset that would transfer to the private sector. In addition, I had long grown weary of the negativity of Customs hierarchy and the failure of the government to effect real, positive change. I thought if I could make something of this case, make a bit of a name for myself, then I could disappear out of the public sector.

I had finished my management diploma, so I now had a university-level degree which, although I studied at Birkbeck, was accredited to University of London. I was considering doing a full- or part-time MBA to lubricate my way into the private sector.

This was all going through my mind. We had the Foreign Office, which meant the government, the New Zealand state and two of its biggest firms – Anchor and the New Zealand Dairy Board – and who knew who else all wanting this to go away. But, after hearing the *Rainbow Warrior* story and buoyed by the auditor's intelligence and the damning evidence we had found, I thought, sod this, let's get justice done here for once.

I was determined to fight this corporate and executive greed as hard as I could.

CHAPTER 22

‖‖‖‖‖‖‖‖‖‖‖‖‖‖‖‖‖‖‖‖‖‖‖‖‖‖‖‖‖‖‖‖‖‖‖‖‖

A storm brewing

In a case where the evidence was this overwhelming there should have been no debate. In any other situation we would have gone in and arrested the executives. When you're dealing with powerful companies with friends in high places and suspected commercial fraud on this scale, however, things weren't that simple.

Nick told me the feeling among the hierarchy was that it was best to just invite the executives into Custom House for a low-key interview.

'Who else would get that treatment on a case like this?' I asked. 'If you go down to the local builder and nick him for a VAT fraud, you don't ring him up and say: "Do you mind coming to Customs next week and having a chat?" You just arrest him and drag him in.'

'We have enough evidence to arrest these people,' I insisted. 'They have to be arrested. One, because it's fair. If you've deprived someone of their liberty, you've arrested them, legally anyway, whether you tell them that or not. If you stop them leaving a room you've arrested them, even if you don't arrest them under the law.'

'When we put these documents to them, what happens if they just get up and walk out the room, if they've not been

239

arrested?' I asked. 'How's that going to sound on tape? Are we then going to arrest them? If we do, we're going to sound like real amateurs, because everything will be taped.'

My other argument was that, for any interview, they would arrive all lawyered up.

'What if, when the going gets tough, they simply say: "My clients are not prepared to talk anymore, thank you and goodnight." We can't do it like that. They've got to be arrested.'

I wanted the shock of the arrest, wanted to do it in front of their colleagues in the office and the factory.

'Oh no, we don't want that,' Nick said.

I offered a compromise. What if we asked them to come into Custom House at an agreed date and time, and then we arrested them?

By this time, Anchor's City lawyers had been in touch. I found it interesting that they were civil lawyers from the same firm who had given Verschuren the tax advice on his butter imports. This was a criminal case, however. I felt we would have the upper hand. Also, they seemed to be representing the company, the New Zealand Dairy Board and all six suspects. Surely there was a conflict of interest there?

Nick and Cedric agreed to this plan. I was relieved. It felt an important argument to win. Despite the pressure we were under, not arresting them would have been ridiculous, and I was glad nobody had again told me to drop it. We were proceeding. That said, I knew Cedric and Nick were worried and wanted to rein me in.

I was determined, however, and was proposing nothing more than what we had been taught back in our BITs course. The advice then, when faced with people who are lords of their environment, was to bring them down to nothing. Strip them of their confidence and show them you had the upper hand. We had that opportunity.

In April 1997, the six executive managers we summoned to Custom House were Monny Verschuren, Alan Absolon, Fernando Guerra – the managing director of Anchor in the UK – Jens Haughstrup, Gualb Sharma and Colin Bell. All of the executives were unequivocal, this was an innocent administrative error made by an Anchor Customs clerk.

Verschuren came first on day one and arrived with a civil solicitor, appearing nervous. I arrested him, read him his rights and he confirmed he understood the caution. Then, I set the tape rolling and asked for his personal details and New Zealand Dairy Board employment history. We'd sent them copies of some of the relevant documents in advance, so now it was his chance to explain.

It was all a misunderstanding, he suggested. He couldn't recall getting the document from his Danish colleague, saying what they were doing was fraudulent. He also denied that he knew that much about the import declarations, and appeared to blame the Customs clerk at Anchor for any errors. He could have remained silent, but that doesn't look good in front of a jury.

I asked if he was the chief executive.

He said he was.

I asked how much he earned.

He disclosed a figure in the region of £80,000 a year.

I asked how much his Customs clerk earned.

'£13,000 a year,' he replied.

'Salary is usually an accurate reflection of responsibility,' I said. I was sure the clerk was good at his job and my Swindon colleagues had confirmed this. 'But I didn't see his name on any of the emails we found.'

At this point he said nothing, and I wasn't surprised; I wasn't expecting him to make an admission.

Their lawyer complained, saying we were being too aggressive, but what did he expect? We were Customs, investigating a potential large-scale commercial fraud.

We didn't manage to get through a great deal. He refused to budge from their position, which was that it was down to simple transactional errors. The interview ended with Verschuren denying everything.

It was going to be a long process. There were lots more documents we wanted to put to them, so I told him to come back the following morning to resume the interviews. They agreed.

In the morning, though, I got a call from Neil Gerrard, from the Manchester office of the big national firm of solicitors, Dibb Lupton Alsop. He was an ex-policeman who, after suffering a serious injury while on traffic duty, used his compensation to retrain as a solicitor. He was exactly the lawyer we did not want. Gone was the Oxbridge, City civil lawyer, in his place was a street fighter.

'Mark, how you doing, mate?' he said, as though we'd been best friends for years. 'I'm now representing the companies and their executives on this matter.'

I knew we'd had too easy a ride yesterday.

He asked for a few weeks to go through the material and bring himself up to speed. He'd then bring his guys back for interview.

'I'll speak to my boss,' I said.

My bosses agreed. In the interests of justice, we couldn't expect a new defence lawyer to pick this up in ten minutes, but I couldn't help feeling that anyone else with our evidence would already have held a few formal interviews and been in court.

By rights, we could have arrested them the day after the raid, or even straight away on the day if we thought there was a chance of evidence going missing. There wasn't. The computer back-up disc had seen to that.

Eight weeks later they were ready to return. This time they also brought with them a Customs consultant from KPMG, George Smith, an ex-investigator, who used to be a member of the ID. We were facing a very different battle now.

We had a development on our side. Martin Sinclair, the senior officer on the Whiskies I didn't always see eye to eye with, had joined Customs B, the division that looked after alcohol, but came to help me with the interviews.

For this type of interrogation, you must be double-handed, and the reality was only I had the full knowledge of the case to be able to know which documents were relevant.

When we invited them back in, we agreed I would lead all the interviews, and Martin would help and advise me. As these were formal, tape-recorded interviews, in the presence of lawyers, Martin was on his best behaviour. Although I wasn't working for him directly, he saw what a good case it was and proved helpful. He told me when to tone it down and said when I was being too aggressive.

Again, Verschuren came in first.

'You're talking too much in the interviews,' Martin told me during one break. 'Just put the documents to them.'

I was so motivated and focused, but the adrenalin was flowing, so it helped that Martin was detached from the case.

At one stage, he said: 'Just stop, talk less, you're giving them a chance to talk themselves out of this.'

And so, with each suspect, we simply put the documents to them, asked them what their explanation was and left it at that. We would let the jury decide whether they believed them or not.

We continued over the next few days. All the executives were remarkably calm and assured. There were some whose names appeared on many documents, so had more at stake, but they were equally as composed. They were also phenomenally well prepared – beyond, I felt, what even the best lawyers could train them. Nothing fazed them or made them sweat or blink. I mainly put it down to their professionalism and confidence in their lawyer's ability to make this all go away, but I couldn't shake the feeling that there was something else at play. I couldn't put my finger on what that could be, though.

We did up to seven 45-minute tapes for each of the suspects, which might not sound much, but I took Martin's view on board and just put the main documents that were relevant to them and asked for their response, as well as general background questions to establish their knowledge and usual working operations.

It was a daunting process. The only formal training I had was that month-long BITs course back when I joined the ID, so I was still learning on the job. It was my first case in charge and my biggest fear was making a mistake and saying something that might mean they got off on a technicality.

I was fortunate because my colleagues in Swindon had done a very good job and the auditors in Luxembourg proved to be brilliant. They gave me the full background to the EU law, and why it was drafted the way it was. It was very arcane and technical; a combination of EU and UK law and it was useful to understand why it was promulgated.

But, while it was easy to become overwhelmed, I reminded myself that Customs had prosecuted commercial frauds for hundreds of years. It was our laws we were enforcing. Most things we did fell under the Customs and Excise Management Act 1979, the Drug Trafficking Offences Act 1986, which applied to police or Customs, or the newly formed Serious Fraud Office, plus EU and VAT law.

There was essentially no difference to smuggling a watch or food stuffs. It was all commercial fraud, charged under section 170 of the Customs and Excise Act, which was being knowingly concerned in the fraudulent evasion of a prohibition or tax, here underpinned by European legislation.

The offence was the Customs declaration. For ordinary members of the public, it is when they walk through the green or red channel at an airport. For Anchor, it was when they filled in a C18 form, called a Customs Declaration. It was like they had come through the green channel with a load of butter. They signed that form saying what they were importing into the UK met all the legal criteria, when that was not the case.

It took us a week to get through the interviews. Their defence, essentially, was that it was an error on the part of the import clerk in Swindon. Their disclosure, they claimed, was unprompted and it was purely coincidence that they made it after the customs officer contacted them.

We weren't permitted to put the legally privileged material to them, but it was in our minds. You can't expunge that, so I put the question to them: 'When you got the test results what actions did you take?'

They didn't say anything that might incriminate themselves. I was hoping they'd say, 'we called our lawyers', and that would have given me an opportunity for further questions and might have led to me getting that aspect before a jury. They didn't. Gerrard had prepped them too well.

Their defence was basically that any irregularities were tiny and a trade matter, their Anchor clerk was careless, and they had reported to us when the problems were found. That didn't fly. It was duty evasion, therefore fraud and a criminal offence.

When we had completed the interviews, I got the tapes transcribed by our typing team and then took them home for a week to check the typing against what was said. It took me that long to check and correct each one against what the stenographer typed. Any changes had to be clearly marked with a bold red for the defence to view the first drafts as unused material. I worked seven straight fifteen-hour days to get them ready to send to the Solicitors' Office. We had been consulting with them throughout, given the size of the case.

That wasn't always the case with Customs. Most cases didn't involve the solicitors. With most drug cases, it is the investigators who decide how they are progressing, and the suspects are arrested and charged that day, without the Solicitors' Office even knowing about it. The case officer goes to the magistrates' court appearance the following day and addresses the bench. The investigator is police and prosecutor; you're completely on your own.

Looking for back up, the Solicitors' Office sent the material on to a junior barrister at Bell Yard chambers in London. That was a sign of how seriously we were still taking the investigation because, although the executives had been released on bail, in the interests of justice we had to decide fairly quickly whether we were going to charge them or not.

While the barrister read through the evidence and assessed the strength of the case, I had other things to consider. There was a strong possibility we might have to go out to New Zealand to interview Dairy Board members there. There was also the

Danish connection, because Anchor supplied its butter products there too, getting a refund from the EU for ingredients like butter and sugar when the biscuits were eventually exported out of Europe. This really was having your cake and eating it. So, I looked into sending a *commission rogatoire* to the Danes, to exchange material and determine compliance there.

In any normal organisation, someone dealing with a case of this magnitude would be given resources to help or, at the very least, the time to concentrate solely on such a big investigation. In Customs that wasn't the case. Right at the time I should've been focusing on preparing for the biggest court date of my career, I was wrenched from my desk to perform duties expected of a very junior investigator.

| | |

The National Investigation Service (NIS) was in turmoil. It was now far too big for our managers – not one of whom had any formal management qualifications – to handle. The culture clash between ex-ID and collection investigators was palpable. A good example was Dover collection, where previously their officers were able to take advantage of £20,000-a-year overtime. This created an 'available anytime' culture. Now, that had been reduced to match our £10,000 annual allowance, where an attitude of 'shirk as much as you can' was in effect. In fact, prior to the ID takeover, my first ACIO from DFIB led the so-called consultation exercise with the collections and ourselves. When I heard him talk about 'blue sky thinking' and mention other corporate buzzwords I knew we were in trouble.

Our bosses could barely run a bath, never mind manage an organisation responsible for recovering multi-millions in taxes every year, engage fairly with the criminal justice system and be officers of the courts. None had any management qualifications or proper training.

A scandal involving some of Customs' most experienced investigators was brewing. This, combined with a cheap booze and fags crisis and the over-zealous claims of a chairwoman eager to please, meant a perfect storm was heading our way. It was to have everlasting repercussions, not just for me but for the entire Customs service.

CHAPTER 23

Getting out

If Customs had been fighting a war on drugs during the eighties, come the nineties it was booze.

The introduction of the European single trade market in 1993 had sparked a tidal wave of smugglers bringing cheap alcohol back into the country from France. The situation got so bad it was impossible to hire a white van in the UK. They were all busy going to Dover every day, getting the ferry to Calais, being loaded up at the supermarkets there and coming straight back.

Who could blame people? With French alcohol taxed at 5 per cent and the UK's at 55, why not head over there?

Organised gangs were also making a killing. They were going to bonded warehouses, where the tax on goods subject to excise duty was zero, and if exported outside the EU, remained duty-free, and falsifying the documents. Instead of taking it to Dover to ship abroad they were stamping it with fake approval showing receipt in non-EU countries and selling it on in the UK. The goods never went near the M25, never mind the ports. They were pocketing millions of pounds of duty. The problem was so big it began destabilising the tax base. Billions of pounds were going missing.

Around the same time our lawyers were considering whether to charge the New Zealand Dairy Board executives, the Customs chairwoman Dame Valerie Strachan was being summoned to parliament to answer questions about the rise in booze smuggling. She told them we had it under control.

That wasn't strictly true – but all available resources were channelled in to fight the problem in a desperate attempt to make it so. Half of London's investigators were taken off drug teams to do it. Everybody's cases got interfered with. Customs chiefs even ordered Alpha off drugs and onto cracking the booze gangs.

One moment I was working on preparing evidence for the Solicitors' Office, the next I got word that Customs B needed our help tracking a booze lorry.

What didn't help was that, in the intervening period, Nick had moved teams. My new boss, Stewart Hollis, did not share Nick's interest in the Anchor case. I think he was terrified it might damage his career. So, whenever Customs B needed help, he ordered me off the case to join in the surveillance. That's how I found myself following a lorry from London to Birmingham.

Another job I was sent on concerned a bonded warehouse in east London, called City Bond. When a lorry departed, I was to follow it. It turned out Henry Black, our old Secret Squirrel from the Uniforms, was now working for Customs B, and had a participating informant inside the warehouse, supplying intelligence on the gang operating from there. It was infuriating. I was trying to keep on top of the Anchor case and had the Solicitors' Office on my back daily, but my time was spent watching a warehouse or following a lorry.

At one stage I lost the rag at Stewart, shouting: 'I need some fucking help here!'

I was feeling the pressure from all sides. To be fair, he did eventually get Tony, a jolly junior officer from Manchester, to help me out by acting as exhibits officer and cataloguing and adducing the evidence needed for court.

Finally, in late spring 1997, there was a breakthrough. David Joseph, a lawyer from the Solicitors' Office had been assigned the case and he arranged a conference in his office with the barrister, Stewart and me.

The barrister said all six should be charged with conspiracy to evade the quota and import duties. He also wanted to indict the executive in New Zealand who was on the emails about this matter and had clear knowledge of the butter tests and related imports here. We were going to charge all seven with conspiracy to evade EU and national Customs law.

Verschuren, New Zealand Dairy Board's highest ranking official in Europe, would be facing six charges of breaching the Customs and Excise Act 1979. The others were going to be charged with three offences.

The charges related to the dates we could prove they were involved, so although we suspected it went on for far longer, we concentrated on the last two years for the criminal case. In tandem, Swindon Excise would quantify all suspect imports going back seven years and issue a demand for back taxes. This eventually reached close to £300 million.

After the Solicitors' Office conference, David drafted the charges and I quickly arranged for all the suspects to come to Wood Street Police Station in the City of London a few days later to be charged, for an appearance the following day at nearby Guildhall Magistrates' Court.

Even though the case was progressing as I had hoped, I was still concerned the Foreign Office might put pressure on us to drop the charges.

The night before the court hearing I went to a public phone

box and rang up *The Times*. I asked for the crime desk and said to the journalist who picked up: 'If you want a good story, make sure you're at Guildhall magistrates' court tomorrow at 10am.'

I didn't give them any private information. I said, with some hyperbole: 'Make sure you cover it. It's a front-pager.'

When the executives appeared in court, all pleaded not guilty and were granted conditional bail. We didn't think they were a flight risk, and having them sitting in prison would have made the clock tick much faster, because we would have only had a set time before we would have to bring them to trial. A case like this would take years to come to trial.

The Times picked up on the case, and from that moment on it went global. I was getting calls from New Zealand and even Danish radio, who were interested in Jens, their countryman. In New Zealand, news of the arrests and the court appearance were greeted with dismay and anger in some quarters. They saw it as part of some European conspiracy to harm the country's exports.

Despite it becoming global news, I was still worried. And I had reason to be. Not long after the court date, a Customs commissioner called me to a meeting in the headquarters. He was a board member and former investigator, Terry Byrne, who had a reputation as a legend in the ID, forged after he jumped onto the wing of an aeroplane full of gear to stop it taking off. He was supposed to be the best investigator the service ever had and the only to have made it onto the board. Unlike most of the commissioners and board members, who were fast-tracked as civil service high-flyers, he had worked his way up from the frontline, through the ID. Terry's title was Director-General for Law Enforcement, and he was responsible for all investigations, prosecutions and civil cases for back taxes. He wanted to know the full details of the case and the strength of the evidence.

As far as I was aware, this was unheard of, so I couldn't help feeling the Foreign Office had been meddling again. Had they realised we were not going to move and went higher up, perhaps even to the chairwoman? I was a bit apprehensive, but once he realised the strength of the case, he seemed fully supportive. I got the sense that the situation had become even more political, but the board didn't want to be seen to be interfering with justice. That said, there were no words of praise or encouragement.

As we approached the committal hearing in July, Neil Gerrard asked me for a meeting. He said he wanted to look over the unused material, such as the original interview transcripts, which I had changed and amended with red pen. He wanted to get his assistant, Karen, who had joined him at the interviews, to make sure there were no discrepancies and analyse all our material.

He came into Custom House to discuss how best to proceed. Then he came to the main reason for his visit. He offered to do a deal on behalf of his clients. His clients were both the six defendants and the New Zealand Dairy Board, which, to me, was a potential conflict of interest. Just as I'd suspected it was with BCCI and Baakza, their interests might not necessary be completely aligned. I was surprised the executives didn't have their own lawyers, rather than the one that represented the company. On the other hand, perhaps they wanted someone, like Lyndon B. Johnson said of J. Edgar Hoover, 'inside the tent pissing out, than outside the tent pissing in'.

He offered to do a compound deal – but there was a condition. He wanted to compound an offence of an untrue declaration, under section 167 of the Customs and Excise Management Act. That means it is an absolute offence – it's a false declaration, it's a crime, but without *mens rea*, a guilty mind. In other words, he wanted to do a deal to a lesser offence, one that only carried a maximum two-year sentence, as opposed to seven years for the most serious crimes.

He made it clear this was an off-the-record conversation, just to find out if, in principle, we were open to a deal.

In some ways I was delighted. I admit to taking some satisfaction seeing him come asking for a deal. They must have known we had a strong case. I knew if I went back to the bosses with this they would force me to take it. Maybe they would be right. A lot of people in my position would take it, but I was determined this case was going to be different.

It was the biggest case the commercial fraud team had ever done, against the most high-profile company. We couldn't just let this go. These things didn't just happen by accident. What about natural justice? What about the restaurant owner who didn't declare his full VAT? They're not going to get this opportunity.

If we agreed to their deal, they'd admit there was a mistake and they'd pay a penalty. It would go down as a crime, but there are degrees of criminality. As far as the executives went, they wouldn't be personally penalised. They wouldn't get a criminal record. The company would pay the penalty for them.

We hadn't charged the company or the New Zealand Dairy Board, but we hadn't ruled it out. We were still looking to either go to New Zealand or begin the extradition process for the executive there. I knew I would have to give the offer some thought – and consider whether to tell the hierarchy. I said we'd think about it and get back to him.

I gave it a few hours, then said: 'No.' I then also had to explain some law to him. To make our routine enquiries on this and all cases, we had to formally tell British Telecom (as they were known then), local councils, HM Land Registry, the banks and utility companies and all the others that assisted us that we were investigating serious crime. This was defined as having a prison sentence above two years. I told him we couldn't lessen the offence the executives were facing, or we could, but I didn't want to.

The offer was easy to turn down. It mattered a great deal to me, it was in the interest of fairness, justice and taxpayers to proceed to court, which would also act as a massive deterrent to other dodgy companies. I didn't tell my boss or Cedric about the offer. I knew what they would say. I wanted to test how the case would pan out.

|||

The committal hearing was slated for July. We packaged our documents, witness statements, transcripts of the tapes and anything else relevant into a bundle and sent it to the Solicitor's Office to serve on the defence and send to the magistrates' court.

We had to persuade the court that these defendants should be sent to the crown court for a major trial.

There are two forms of committal – contested, where defendants plead not guilty and say they want to test the evidence, or uncontested, when they don't oppose the case and it sails through to the crown court. That's what the New Zealand Dairy Board defendants did. It was an uncontested committal.

I wasn't privy to their thinking. Perhaps they thought it was clear the evidence was so strong they would have lost if they had contested it. One cynical consideration was what the lawyers stood to gain if it went to a full trial. They would certainly earn millions more, but what else? Prestige? A career move to the capital and the legal Premier League? RAC club membership? I didn't know.

With the case progressing to the crown court, in the grand scheme of things, my job was done. An investigator's main concern is to get their case committed. The issues over additional charges, or extra evidence and extradition were largely for the bosses and lawyers to decide.

Once more the case made front page news in the *Financial Times* and was again picked up globally. In New Zealand the reaction was, once more, one of incredulity. I don't think people could believe UK Customs were taking on the nation's Dairy Board.

It sent out such a strong signal to other companies that we were not to be messed with. For the first time, we had arrested top people, taken them to court and not just rolled over when they came begging with their cheque book wide open.

It should have been the beginning of something big. It should have been a time when Customs were being talked about for all the right reasons. We should have been enjoying having an increase in resources coming our way, so we could carry out more controls on other big companies and see who else was evading tax.

I should have been basking in the afterglow of a job well done, been able to take my pick of the biggest and best investigations and really made a name for myself.

That's what should have happened; none of it did.

Before the year was out, I had left Customs. After twelve years, I had finally had enough and, with this case, had had several tempting offers from the private sector. I jumped at one of them.

I could also smell the stench of a rotting Customs corpse, and I was right. The end was coming for the Investigation Service – and for Customs as an independent outfit for hundreds of years. Everything was falling apart.

EPILOGUE

A disabled grandad, in his seventies, was left stranded in a French port with his son-in-law. Their car was confiscated. In it was the old man's walking stick. His crime? Customs officers didn't believe the amount of alcohol they were trying to take over to the UK was for 'personal use'. In the crackdown on booze smuggling, anyone became fair game. Cars were seized at the ports – and then sold off for as little as £20. Meanwhile, in a VAT clampdown, dozens of small businesses were targeted in what was little more than bureaucratic bullying.

As we entered the 21st century, these were deemed Customs' priorities. Meanwhile, on Britain's streets, drugs smuggled in from Asia, Africa and mainland Europe had never been in greater supply. The price plummeted for cocaine and heroin, such was the flow of drugs into the country. At the same time, billions of pounds of tax and excise duties were being evaded. In the burgeoning mobile phone and computer industries, VAT fraud had become so lucrative that organised criminals were making it their crime of choice. Reminiscent of the time when armed robbers turned to drugs, now gangs saw commercial fraud as a rich stream of income to mine.

It all begged the question – what the hell was happening with HM Customs and Excise?

One of the first significant attempts to shake things up came when Richard Broadbent, a 46-year-old former merchant banker, was brought in to replace the beleaguered Dame Valerie as chairman of the board. He revamped the management structure at Customs to supposedly improve things, but left in 2003, and by then the image of the service was already taking a battering.

The latest TV drama to glamorise the work of the ID, ITV's *The Knock*, had only recently ended its run after five series. Following on from the successes of *The Collectors* and *The Duty Men*, it fictionalised life in the London City and South Collection Investigation Unit. But while on-screen Customs officers were once again seen as the pin-up boys of law enforcement, on the streets the reality was much different.

Ironically, officers didn't even call the raids 'the knock' anymore. Following SAS covert ops training, it was now called 'the slaughter', as though that mattered. Yet that small change seemed indicative of the reforms that had swept through the service since I left in 1997. While drugs flooded the streets, causing nationwide crime and health problems, and gangs flouted tax laws with impunity, Customs almost appeared so consumed by its own scandals that it was powerless to react to the new wave in crime.

When I joined the Investigation Division it was 1,000-strong, with another thousand in local units spread around the country. The beginning of the end came when the national team took over the regional operations. The move angered the local offices, while at the same time pressure was growing from the police and intelligence services to claim jurisdiction over the investigations Customs were doing. The final nail in the Investigation Division's coffin came when a major operation into alcohol tax fraud collapsed, and then the unthinkable happened – the police launched Operation Gestalt, and arrested Customs officers during the crackdown on booze smuggling, following whistleblowing by a Customs solicitor.

It all blew up at the London City Bond (LCB) warehouse in the East End, where Henry Black had been running an informant. He was being tipped off about criminals who were coming to the bonded warehouse, taking the booze tax-free, claiming it was for exporting and therefore not subject to excise duties, but then selling it on in the UK. Henry's participating informant gave the produce to the smugglers, then rang Henry to say they had just left and provided details of their location.

Instead of stopping the fraud, Henry and other Customs investigators let the lorries run, in an attempt to catch the major criminals behind it. Letting the booze leave LCB ran up huge losses. It was said these reached an eye-watering £2 billion.

They eventually rounded up scores of bootlegger criminals. But Henry, or his colleagues, should've disclosed how they received the intelligence, under the court rules of providing unused material. Perhaps it was because there would have been repercussions for him, or perhaps for another reason, but whatever the reason, they didn't. A key Customs prosecution witness was Alf Allington, managing director of LCB, who gave evidence in numerous trials where he was presented as a 'trade source' – a legitimate businessman doing only what he was obliged to do by law. Under oath, he denied he was an informant or had any knowledge that fraud was taking place. Customs officials knew at the time that both these statements were lies. In fact, as he later confessed, he was the participating informant facilitating the fraud with the knowledge and encouragement of

Customs. It goes back to the concept of an agent provocateur, something I was always uneasy with.

Twenty Customs officials, including Henry and even commissioner Terry Byrne, who I met over the New Zealand Dairy Board case, and Customs' head lawyer David Pickup, were under investigation by the Metropolitan Police. All were suspended, but denied any knowledge. The list contained many of my former colleagues and bosses. Some were arrested.

In 2001, appeal judges ordered a retrial of one case, in which Allington's evidence had helped secure a conviction. The judges found 'a serious failure' by Customs to disclose Allington was a participating informant and the 'extent of their participation in the offences with Customs' encouragement'.

A year later, the appeal court quashed the convictions of eight men, including those who had pleaded guilty. The court found that 'lies' had been told deliberately by Customs to hide Allington's true status from the judge. Basically, Customs were accused of perverting the course of justice. Despite this, though, other prosecutions continued.

In November 2002, an inquiry headed by Mr Justice Butterfield was called into the LCB affair, following the collapse of the last prosecutions. He identified several serious deficiencies within Customs, including a culture of excessive secrecy.

This was illustrated by the fact that Customs even failed to hand over a document, called the LCB Spine, to Butterfield. This was Customs' own detailed internal analysis of the LCB fiasco, charting key events from day one where mistakes might have been made, annotated with comments.

Furthermore, DFIB's covert investigation into London's bureaux de change, which we had started years before, and was still ongoing, also collapsed. Its undercover agents were involved with and tainted by the bootlegging debacle, so couldn't credibly give evidence on a massive money laundering prosecution.

In 2005, Terry Byrne spoke out about the crisis, and said the decision to keep the LCB Spine report from the inquiry was made by Sir Richard Broadbent, the then-chairman of Customs. Byrne called the decision to conceal that Allington was a participating informant 'ridiculous', but he predicted that 'not one single Customs officer will ever be convicted of any criminal offence whatsoever because of their involvement with all of the LCB cases'.

That proved correct. Four years later, the government and its lawyers ordered the police to abandon the investigation into alleged corruption involving the twenty senior Customs officials. The inquiry had cost the taxpayer at least £5.5 million, yet the Crown Prosecution Service said it was not in the public interest to continue, and that there was no realistic chance of a conviction. It was very Orwellian. Of course there was no realistic chance.

Despite no evidence of wrongdoing, none of the officers originally suspended worked for the service again. Terry Byrne retired from Customs in November 2004 on reaching the age of 60. David Pickup became Director General and in 2007 left to become Attorney General of the Falkland Islands Government.

By then the rot had set in. The whole service imploded; they were getting attacked from all sides.

The *Sun* – traditionally a newspaper that stood staunchly behind law enforcement – ran a front-page campaign criticising Customs' booze and fags crackdown of cross-Channel day-trippers. MPs had a go in Parliament. In the end the government announced it was increasing the personal allowances for bringing tobacco and alcohol into Britain, to help differentiate between regular travellers and smugglers. The *Sun* declared victory and, even though the government claimed it had been thinking about raising the allowance for some time, the Customs hierarchy admitted its image had taken a battering.

But that wasn't all. Sensing that the booze informant operations were indicative of a wider culture of corruption, the police began arresting Customs investigators for essentially drug smuggling. The system where officers let controlled deliveries run came under scrutiny. There were allegations that officers were benefitting financially from heroin importations being allowed into the UK, linked to an informant in Karachi.

This was a gravely serious allegation. I might have witnessed unethical, even criminal behaviour by the odd rogue officer, or been aware of low-level rule bending, but there was never a culture of wrongdoing. Going back through history, from the days when Customs officers first used clipper ships, the service had a reputation for robustly upholding the law. It might have been an unpopular and powerful organisation, but it had never suffered from the same stain of corruption that plagued the police. Chaucer, a former duty man, would surely have been turning in his grave.

Three drug investigators stood trial when it was claimed they had set up an illegal operation allowing heroin to be sold on the streets. The jury heard they had allowed at least 1.7 kilos of heroin to be sold in Leeds and Bradford, and had collaborated with a drug smuggler who was on the run at the time. It was also alleged that they permitted heroin suppliers in Pakistan to receive a share of Customs reward money funded by taxpayers, as well as cash from street sales in Britain, and planned how to break rules covering informant handling and undercover smuggling operations.

West Midlands police had investigated nearly a dozen operations during which up to 200 kilos of heroin was imported into Britain because of controlled deliveries. Before the case went to court, eight officers in total from the north of England – and an informant – were facing charges, but the Crown Prosecution Service decided not to proceed against five of them. Tragically, a junior customs investigator killed himself in the wake of the police action, because he feared he was going to be made the scapegoat.

The officers whose charges went ahead – a senior investigator from Leeds, a drug liaison officer in Pakistan and a case officer, all pleaded not guilty to misconduct at Sheffield Crown Court. They were all found guilty by a jury. The police inquiry was launched in 1998, a year after I left, and ran for eight years, spanning three continents.

It was said one of the officers and a regular participating informant met a businessman connected with recovering stolen art and offered him a deal to 'set up' a well-known underworld family with a huge consignment of cocaine, which would be imported from South America by Customs and the informant. But the businessman knew the offer was basically entrapment. He contacted police, who covertly recorded his meeting with the Customs officer.

Police also recorded evidence that the officers allowed a Bradford drug dealer to sell a sample of 1.7 kilos of heroin worth £170,000 to pay suppliers in Pakistan. The method used was the same the officers had tried for the cocaine deal. In total, the operation related to the importation of 35 kilos of heroin worth £3.5 million.

Interestingly, Terry Byrne, whose brother was a senior Customs investigator around this time, was called as a witness in that case, and said it was quite normal for large samples of heroin to be allowed to go on to the streets.

The three officers only received suspended sentences but lost their jobs. The judge clearly didn't agree with the jury and the verdicts were met with anger throughout Customs at the way they were hung out to dry by their senior colleagues.

By an incredible coincidence, in the same month they were convicted, a new crime-fighting agency was announced. The Serious Organised Crime Agency (SOCA) was formed following a merger of the National Crime Squad (NCS), the National Criminal Intelligence Service (NCIS), the National Hi-Tech Crime Unit (NHTCU), the investigative and intelligence sections of Customs on serious drug trafficking, and the Immigration Service's responsibilities for organised immigration crime.

The writing had been on the wall since the mid-nineties, but especially since 1998, when the National Crime Squad was created.

The NCS was a merger of the seven Regional Crime Squads (RCS), made up of detectives seconded from the police. They dealt with drug dealing, armed robberies and high-tech crime. NCS senior management hated Customs, partly because we had been far more effective than the police at penetrating large criminal gangs and partly because we had the power of the writ of assistance. They wanted that unique search warrant.

NCIS was formed in 1992 out of the old National Drugs Intelligence Unit (NDIU), which was part of the Home Office. It was a huge bureaucratic waste of money. It had no powers to launch its own operations, it purely produced reports for the government and analysed the same data and trends that my old team at Strategic Intelligence handled.

The changes spelled the end of Customs and its investigation service as I knew it. The whole agency collapsed. Customs was subsumed into Inland Revenue, and drugs work was farmed out to the National Crime Squad, which was effectively the police.

As an investigation body, Customs went from being one of the best in the world to being disbanded. The demise of such an esteemed service was a damning failure of leadership. Operationally, the Customs teams were second to none in the UK, but it was a case of lions led by donkeys.

When I joined DFIB, the attitude was to bring the best people together to enforce new legislation. It wasn't perfect, we were learning on the job, but it was the right strategy. And then we were side-tracked by government and political interference.

Clearly, the main thrust came from George Bush asking Margaret Thatcher for a favour regarding Manuel Noriega – a link to our BCCI operation that was so secret because nobody wanted it coming out.

I suspect Walter and others got that gig because they'd done other very sensitive work before and could be trusted. They were on the Customs teams that worked cases against the oil companies during the miners' strike. The oil companies had told Thatcher that unless she let them bring in the oil tax-free, they were going to turn off the pipe and the government would have been in real trouble because they were going to lose the strike. The oil companies were shelling out millions in tax every week, but if they could get Thatcher when she was vulnerable, they could use it to their advantage. It's worth remembering that her husband Dennis worked for Burmah Oil; he would have had some influence there too.

Looking back, I think Customs wanted to prosecute the oil firms for not paying tax and only later found out about the dirty deal between them and the government.

Political interference happened all the time, but when they began meddling with the operational side of Customs ID it was a disaster.

In 2006, when SOCA was launched, elements of the press labelled it the British FBI. But would the FBI do away with its most effective tool against organised crime? That's what SOCA did by getting rid of Alpha and its elite tappers, and disbanding the NIS. Alpha used to run several major operations in London at once, seizing an average of 40 kilos of class A drugs every week. In its first year, SOCA ran one operation. Alpha was the best weapon in the war on drugs the UK ever had. If anything, it should've been expanded, not disbanded

SOCA recruited 2,500 investigators from NCS and Customs, but within six months found that they had 400 more than they needed. The recruitment also did little to address the imbalance in diversity when it came to the investigators. There were still too few ethnic minority and female investigators, which would have greatly strengthened the effectiveness of the service. Too often the presence of a single woman on operational teams left Customs open to the criticism of tokenism. Eventually, they did appoint a female ACIO, but not in an operational role, leading to the cruel, but not unjustified comments that she was put in charge of paperclips.

In a further erosion of Customs' powers, they lost the ability to prosecute independently, with the Crown Prosecution Service taking over their cases.

|||

SOCA's role was to target drug trafficking, people smuggling and a hitlist of 130 'Mr Bigs' of UK crime. However, the 'Mr Bigs' hitlist was ridiculed after it emerged some of the 130 were dead, in prison or low-level criminals.

Not long after SOCA was formed, an undercover Customs agent being posted from Ecuador to Colombia lost a memory stick containing the 'crown jewels' of data – the names and codenames, addresses and details of dozens of SOCA officers and drug informants from her old office – while landing at El Dorado Airport in Bogota. While she was recalled to London, the then-Chief Investigator Paul Evans, who had transferred over from MI6, where he was the boss of the secret service's Vienna station, ordered an internal inquiry. Agents and informants had to be relocated and the total cost of aborted operations was £100 million.

These were the sorts of bungles that led to SOCA being criticised in 2009 by Terry Byrne, whose proposals had helped lead to its creation. He said: 'I would not have proposed the transfer of Customs drugs responsibilities and resources to such an organisation if I had known how it was going to be so ill-directed.'

I could see the writing on the wall back in 1997. My case highlighted the issues plaguing the service. In the aftermath of the committal hearing, when I wasn't following lorries out of the bonded warehouse, there was still work to be done on the case. I went out to Aarhus, in Denmark, where a lot of Anchor products were channelled to the EU, and had a *commission rogatoire* to MD Foods there. We also put a similar request to go to New Zealand to try to get evidence and to interview the co-conspirator over there.

If I had stayed, I probably could have gone to New Zealand,

but I knew the government there would block the extradition and we didn't have the power of search in a foreign country. I knew we weren't going to get any help there, so I knew it was going to be a wasted enterprise. That was exactly how it transpired.

The publicity around the case meant my name was getting known. Lee and Allen, forensic accountants, approached me. They were ex-PricewaterhouseCoopers partners, based in Fleet Street. One of them, Tim Allen, was from Sheffield. They wanted to expand their forensic accounting and offer tax advice, but they also had an investigation arm, Quest, which they wanted me to assist with. One of their clients was a premier league club, who wanted to use them to follow prospective players they wanted to sign, to make sure they weren't party animals or had chaotic lifestyles. I decided to take the plunge into the private sector. I had also made up my mind to do an MBA, which I did at Westminster Business School. Lee and Allen were only paying slightly more than Customs, but they also offered a share of their profits.

When I resigned from Customs, Cedric Andrew called me in and offered me all sorts of jobs and an immediate promotion to entice me to stay. He was proposing a double promotion, to SIO, team leader. It was flattering but I had already made up my mind. There wasn't anything he could say to persuade me.

I found, though, that once you left Customs, they viewed you like a turncoat. To them, I was poacher turned gamekeeper. To anyone having problems with Customs, however, I could help.

My first big case was for Tesco. Their intellectual property lawyer had a case where you could buy Levi jeans for £5 in some of Tesco's supermarkets. Levi objected to their jeans being sold off cheaply, and in a supermarket, and argued they did not supply Tesco direct. The supermarket giant acquired them from the grey market. They fought out a war that went to European Court.

Levi found Customs lawyers in the private sector to advise them and get officers to seize any container when it came into the UK. I got a call to investigate and went to Heathrow and managed to get Tesco's container released immediately.

The jeans promotion was part of a multi-million-pound marketing campaign for Tesco, so they were delighted.

During that case, I needed a lawyer and all were conflicted except Neil Gerrard. After being on opposing sides over Anchor, here we were on the same side with Tesco. While he'd now moved to London and joined a Pall Mall club, his assistant Karen was still based in Manchester, and I went for a meeting with her there. She also was from Sheffield and offered to drive me back to the steel city as it was Friday night. We had a long chat and she disclosed something she had seen on the Anchor case.

While she was going through the unused material, she found a document that said I was under investigation for leaking information. I knew nothing about this. Now I was away from Customs and we were working together, she could tell me.

Customs had slipped a note into the unused material that they were investigating me. That was a crime; they were trying to accuse me of wrongdoing.

It transpired that the investigation into me had nothing to do with Anchor. Once I had joined Lee and Allen, I had rung up the British Importers Association (BIA), letting them know that if any of their companies had a problem with Customs they could ring me, because I was now advising them. The BIA sent the message out and one of their members, a textiles company in Nottingham, made a note of my number. By coincidence, Customs raided that firm and found my name in their contacts list. They jumped to the conclusion that I called the company directly and told them to expect a raid. It was complete nonsense. I hadn't had any dealings with the textiles firm.

Customs rang me up and wanted to call me for an interview.

I said: 'If you want to interview me, come and arrest me.'

I went to see my MP Glenda Jackson, the member for Hampstead, and complained about my treatment, which conferred parliamentary privilege in the process. She wrote to the Treasury, who told Customs to back off, which they did. I was shocked at how vindictive they got, and how quickly.

Although Customs went away, in the short term it felt like it was damaging my career. It was being written about in the professional journals. The next thing I knew, Customs went to the Old Bailey and dropped the case against Anchor, blaming me. They said I had made a mistake on the chain of evidence that would prejudice the case. Again, this was absolute nonsense, as we'd had a dedicated exhibits officer, Tony, who dealt with this and produced all exhibits for court in his witness statement. We'd already sailed through committal with no issues. Even Gerrard said publicly this was rubbish.

And this was their second go at me. Prior to this, they'd put to the judge that I'd written a marketing article about Customs, generally, that was prejudicial. What they didn't know was I'd borrowed this from a mate who was a former Customs lawyer, who subsequently left to become a leading tax attorney with a top City firm of solicitors. He'd confirmed in print that I'd asked his permission prior to me publishing.

I assumed the Foreign Office had put pressure on them

again and they decided they didn't want the hassle. They dropped the criminal case but pursued Anchor in a civil case. Interestingly, the following year, the European Court of Auditors issued a report claiming that the New Zealand Dairy Board owed the EU almost NZ$900 million (£463 million) in unpaid import duties from the period 1973 to 1995. Due to a three-year restriction on seeking back duties the claim was limited to NZ$236 million (£121 million). The claim was based on the assertion that the butter imported during this period exceeded butterfat limits and, therefore, was ineligible for New Zealand's preferential tariff. That's how much a search warrant and a bit of bottle was worth.

|||

For years to come, Customs and the New Zealand Dairy Board/ Anchor clashed in court over the unpaid duty. All brands were tarnished by the battle.

In 1999, Anchor Foods faced a demand from Customs to freeze its assets, after the firm planned to sell itself to New Zealand Milk for £9 million. Customs claimed the move was a plan designed to evade around £270 million in import duties. The dispute centred on whether the spreadable butter was a natural product, liable to a duty of £720 per ton, or a processed product like margarine, which attracted a tariff of £2,000 a ton. Customs commissioners claimed the transfer plan was a 'gross undervaluation' of the company and said the true value of the company was between £30 and £100 million. They argued that the transfer appeared to have no other commercial purpose but to rid the company of debt. Anchor always denied this. They argued Customs had misunderstood the nature of the business and claimed it didn't make butter but simply imported, repackaged and distributed the butter produced by New Zealand's farmers.

In 2001, the Dairy Board was merged with the two largest New Zealand dairy cooperatives (which represented 96 per cent of the industry) to a company initially called GlobalCo, but shortly afterwards renamed Fonterra. That still wasn't the end of the story.

It had always struck me how composed the New Zealand Dairy Board executives had been during the interviews – like they knew what was coming, even aside from the material we disclosed ahead of the meetings.

I had put it down to their professionalism, but later I was told that a colleague had allegedly been leaking information about the case and it had got back to Gerrard and so had helped the suspects.

George Smith was the ex-Customs investigator for KPMG. My boss Cedric had a friend, a former Customs investigator from their days in Birmingham ID, who did the same job for another big five rival accountancy firm. It was interesting how the big accountancy firms hired ex-Customs officers and investigators. Gerrard told me Cedric's consultant friend was unhappy KPMG were getting millions from the Anchor case. He was trying to get involved too, based on his contact with Cedric. If Cedric was talking about this case, however innocently, to his friend, who then relayed the information to Gerrard, that could have corrupted our interviews and the whole case. That might have explained how they were so self-assured throughout. Rather than blame me for leaks they might have been better served looking closer to home.

The dispute between Levi and Tesco raged on for two years but, because of my success in freeing their container, I started getting calls from accountancy firms like Ernst & Young and Deloitte, and I went to work for Ernst & Young in their tax department. Interestingly, some of my colleagues were ex-Customs.

By this time, I was speculating in property – or, to be more accurate, in fresh air. Charmian's brother had a friend who was a shrewd property dealer in South London. He became a bit of a mentor to me. He taught us how it was possible to buy commercial properties, apply for permission for change of use and sell them to developers to convert into residential homes. He didn't build or redevelop properties himself, just sold them to builders to convert. Without big cash, I needed a cute strategy, so I started buying the freehold to apartment blocks with flat roofs and then got planning permission to extend the rooftop, so a developer could build extra penthouses. I thought it was amazing. It was, literally, selling fresh air.

I discovered that residents in the blocks with roof space to develop didn't object. Their flats were going to be worth considerably more because aesthetically it made them look nicer, their service charges would be lower as it would be divided between more people, and their heating bills would be reduced because heat would no longer escape through a flat roof.

In a property hotspot, like London was then, the financial returns were massive and relatively quick. We found we could turn around a property sale in twelve months.

After ten years together, Charmian and I drifted apart, and she was mainly in Congo on the trail of blood diamonds. I continued investing in real estate, and I set up a company to promote sustainable development. Besides apartment blocks, I dealt with any previously developed land or brownfield site, including old schools, pubs and petrol stations. I used to walk the streets looking for potential properties, but also found them at auctions and through selling agents. Everything I did was underpinned by the national policy document PPG3, which recommended developers should be building more densely in urban areas, not on greenfield sites. Eventually, it became so lucrative and time-consuming that, in 2001, I left Ernst & Young to focus on it full-time.

Three years later, while at a party a friend had taken me to, I met a beautiful, bubbly and highly intelligent Italian lady called Sara. She was working at the Marsden Hospital. We hit it off and started dating. After a few years together we relocated to Verona, which is where we still live, and have been married for nearly ten years.

While I've left those days of surveillance and snooping around firmly in the past, there are some aspects of my investigator training that will never leave me. For one thing, the advanced driving course comes in very handy when negotiating my way past Italian drivers!

SELECTED SOURCES

The following sources were used to help confirm wider details to various Customs' operations:

Addicott, Cameron, *The Interceptor*, Penguin, 2011

Harris, Phil and Frank McDonald (eds.), *European Business and Marketing*, Sage, 2004

Kerry, John and Hank Brown, *The BCCI Affair: A Report to the Committee on Foreign Relations United States Senate*, 1992

Mazur, Robert, *The Infiltrator: Undercover in the World of Drug Barons and Dirty Banks*, Corgi, 2016

Rijock, Ken, *The Laundry Man*, Penguin, 2013

Walsh, Peter, *Drug War: The Secret History*, Milo, 2020

AP News, 'Akbar, former chief for BCCI's treasury operation, a key figure in BCCI case', 6 September 1991

The New York Times, 'Banker tells how Noriega used BCCI account', 10 December 1991

Washington Post, 'BCCI clients offered prostitutes, Hill told', 19 March 1992

The Times, 'Butter firm loses court tax action', 27 February 1999

Independent on Sunday, 'When to knock: the problem that's exercising Customs', 17 November 2002

Tampa Bay Times, 'Six convicted in BCCI case', 17 October 2005

Guardian, 'Former Customs officers face jail for illegal heroin operation', 8 April 2006

Guardian, 'After 256 days in court, the judge's verdict: a hopeless, incoherent farce', 13 April 2006

Daily Mail, 'Butter ban', 17 July 2006

Guardian, 'Files close on BCCI banking scandal', 17 May 2012

Sunday Times, 'How a bank almost sank the Hebrides', 18 September 2016

Daily Telegraph, 'Breaking the bad guys' money laundering game', 31 August 2016

ACKNOWLEDGEMENTS

I would like to thank my agent Andrew Lownie for seeing the potential in this project.

To Douglas Wight, thank you for all your help throughout the process.

Thank you to Ellen Conlon for the faith you've shown in this book, your infectious enthusiasm and skilful editing.

And to all the team at Icon Books, I am truly grateful for the fantastic job you've done in publishing this book.